the simple guide to CATS

Sandra Toney
&
Kelli A. Wilkins

t.f.h.
T.F.H. Publications, Inc.

© 2003

Distributed in the UNITED STATES to the Pet Trade by T.F.H. Publications, Inc., 1 TFH Plaza, Neptune City, NJ 07753; on the Internet at www.tfh.com; in CANADA by Rolf C. Hagen Inc., 3225 Sartelon St., Montreal, Quebec H4R 1E8; Pet Trade by H & L Pet Supplies Inc., 27 Kingston Crescent, Kitchener, Ontario N2B 2T6; in ENGLAND by T.F.H. Publications, PO Box 74, Havant PO9 5TT; in AUSTRALIA AND THE SOUTH PACIFIC by T.F.H. (Australia), Pty. Ltd., Box 149, Brookvale 2100 N.S.W., Australia; in NEW ZEALAND by Brooklands Aquarium Ltd., 5 McGiven Drive, New Plymouth, RD1 New Zealand; in SOUTH AFRICA by Rolf C. Hagen S.A. (PTY.) LTD., P.O. Box 201199, Durban North 4016, South Africa; in Japan by T.F.H. Publications. Published by T.F.H. Publications, Inc.

Contents

Why Own a Cat? P. 17

The Cat Fanciers' Association p. 45

How to Spot
a Healthy
Feline
p. 64

Feline
Veterinarians
p. 75

Different Types of Cat Litter p. 104

Grooming Tools
p. 115

Urinary Tract Problems p. 159

Chapter 14: In Case of Emergency

Senior
Diets
p. 175

Should You Breed Your Cat? p. 209

Best Friends
Animal
Sanctuary
p. 230

Part One
So You Want a
Cat or Kitten

"Okay, time's up. It's my turn on the windowsill."

Should You Get a Cat?

So you've decided it's time to enrich your life by adopting a pet but cannot determine which type of furry animal you want to share your precious time with. Whether you had a loving pet cat as a childhood companion, admired a stray kitten that occasionally hung around your back door, or heard heartwarming kitty stories from your friends and co-workers, you are now wondering if a feline, with all its independent and somewhat "meticulous" habits, would suit your lifestyle. Is a cat the right pet for you?

Choosing Between Cats and Dogs

Since felines replaced canines as America's number one pet several years ago, their number, as well as their popularity, has steadily soared. There are

Is a cat the right pet for you?

Pet Population Continues to Grow

The results of the United States Pet Food Institute survey released in 2001 shows that the US pet cat and dog populations continued to grow. The number of pet cats is over 75 million, while the number of dogs grew from 59 million to 60 million. Obviously, cats are still the "top dog!"

Cats will enjoy some quiet time when you are away.

approximately 60 million cats living among us and with us in our households. Obviously, there is something agreeable about owning a cat.

The one element that has most likely shifted many pet owners to preferring cats over dogs is the fact that they are fairly self-sufficient, particularly in the bathroom department. With the busy and active lifestyles of most individuals and families today, being home to walk the dog whenever he gets the urge (assuming he is a house dog and can't go outside) is sometimes impossible.

If you have an important meeting or dinner date immediately after school or work, it may not be possible for you to go to your house and take the dog outside to do his business—which can lead to quite a mess for you to clean up when you do make it home.

Your self-sufficient cat, however, does not need to be walked or let outside to potty because (if trained properly) your indoor kitty will automatically use her litter box when the need arises, without having to wait for your arrival.

If you have to leave the house for long periods of time, the guilt of leaving an inside dog home alone is enough to gnaw at your conscience. Most dogs love being in your company and the looks of loss and sorrow as you pull out of your driveway can melt any heart. Dogs can suffer from severe separation anxiety and sometimes become quite destructive when you are away for periods of time.

Your cat, however, will probably sleep the entire time you are away, leaving you feeling somewhat less guilty (but still a little guilty, nonetheless) at the thought of a furry friend waiting anxiously for your return. Pets cannot be categorized, though. While one cat might not care if you are gone all day, another might miss your companionship terribly.

There are several other reasons why many Americans are choosing to own cats instead of dogs. Available living space and housing conditions are often considerations in determining the right pet for an individual. Cats take up less room than dogs. If the potential pet owner is living in an apartment or small condo, there may not be enough space to raise a dog. A cat can, however, readily adapt to life in a small apartment and may even relish the cozy atmosphere, making the apartment her "world."

Cats are quiet, clean animals and are often welcomed in places where other pets are banned. For example, some apartment complexes have pet restrictions and many do not allow dogs for various reasons. Usually the management or landlord will make an exception to the "no pet" rule and allow cats in the building as long as they are kept indoors. When bringing any pet into your home, make sure you have ample room for your new friend so she can play and exercise, yet not infringe on the living space of the other family members.

If necessary, a cat can be left alone for a day or two as long as food, water, and a clean litter box are provided. Cats sleep an average of 12 to 18 hours a day and may not even notice that you've been gone long. In fact, your cat might even welcome the solitude! If a dog owner needs to be away

Cats take up less living space than most dogs.

On average, cats sleep between 12 and 18 hours a day.

Part 1

How Long do Cats Really Sleep?

Cats generally sleep anywhere from 12 to 18 hours a day. About three and one-half hours of this sleep is called R.E.M. sleep (Rapid Eye Movement sleep) which is a type of very deep sleep. The brain is most active during this stage of sleep. The remaining hours of a cat's sleep cycle are spent in a sort of cat "napping" state—meaning the cat remains partially alert to his or her surroundings.

A cat makes a warm, loving companion.

from home for a weekend, or even overnight, he will often have to rely on a friend or neighbor to come over several times to walk the dog. This can become a nuisance to friends and family members who are called upon to "dogsit."

Overall, cat owners have less to be concerned with regarding their felines. They don't have to worry about their cats chasing the mailman or barking for hours if they're left alone. Cats are self-reliant creatures that can take care of many of their basic needs without the "help" of humans. This independence does not make them cold and aloof, however. Cats are warm, affectionate creatures that have become our companions by choice, not by necessity.

Cat Considerations

There are many factors to take into consideration when getting a feline. Cats come in all shapes and sizes. How do you choose the best pet for your lifestyle? Ask yourself the following questions before starting your search for the perfect pet.

√ Do you want a purebred cat or a "regular" household cat (also known as a Moggie or mixed breed)?

√ What will the cat's role be in the family? (Will she be a household pet and companion, or do you plan on entering her in cat shows?)

√ How much money do you want to spend on your cat? (Purebreds are often considerably more expensive than mixed breeds, but their lineage can be traced back for several generations. Mixed breed cats can be obtained for a small fee at many animal shelters and pet adoption agencies.)

√ Where will you get your cat? There are many options available, including breeders, animal shelters, pet rescue organizations, pet shops, and private owners.

√ Do you want a cat or a kitten? Kittens are lovable little bundles of playful trouble, but they grow up quickly. They are quite a handful as they learn and explore the world around them.

√ Will you have time to train and "babysit" your new pet? Adult cats are just as affectionate as kittens and have already settled into the world; they know what is expected of them and are generally more sedate.

√ How much time do you want to spend grooming your cat? Believe it or not, that can factor into your decision. Long-haired breeds such as Persians and Maine Coons will require more grooming than short-haired breeds such as the Siamese or the Abyssinian. Long-haired breeds may need to be brushed and combed daily or several times a week.

Once you've decided on the type of cat you want, you need to prepare for the responsibility that lies ahead.

A Lifetime of Love

Choosing to share your life with any pet is a big commitment and not something to be entered into lightly. You must be sure that you will be able to provide food and shelter, medical care, and plenty of love for the rest of its days for whatever pet you decide to become a parent and companion to.

Kittens are curious about their new world.

Bringing a new pet into your home is a big responsibility.

Cats can live up to 20 years, so think carefully about all aspects of pet ownership before you bring a cat into your life. The cat will be a family member for many years to come and will require almost as much attention and care as would a child.

Often, the initial purchase of the cat is considerably less than the costs involved in maintaining the cat throughout her lifetime. You can now consider yourself a "parent" to the cat and will have to provide everything your feline needs to live a full life: food, shelter, cat litter, toys, and all the necessary medical checkups and vaccinations.

Your cat will not only depend on you financially, but will also depend on you emotionally. Be sure you have enough time to devote to taking care of your feline and making her feel like a valued member of the family. Even though cats are "independent" they need and thrive on attention from their owners. Will you take time every day to play with your cat? Groom her at least once a week? Let her curl up on your lap while you watch television and maybe even let her sleep in your bed? Your cat will be counting on you to keep her safe and happy for the rest of her life. Be sure you are up to this rewarding responsibility.

Your cat will depend on you for all her needs.

Sharing your life with a cat will make coming home more enjoyable each day. Waking up with a pair of green, blue, or gold feline eyes gazing into yours will make getting out of bed in the morning just a little bit easier. Deciding to get a cat–no matter what age, size, purebred, or mix–should be a happy and exciting time for you and your family.

Once you've made that crucial decision to own a cat (well, actually, the cat will probably think that she owns you), you will wonder how you ever lived without a cat in your world in the first place. And one thing is for certain–you will never want to experience life without a cat again. Adopting a cat means adopting a happier, more fulfilling existence.

Other Household Members

Another important aspect to consider when deciding if you should get a cat is its potential impact on the other family

Part 1

Statistics From the CDC on Animal Bites

According to a study conducted by the Center for Disease Control and Prevention (CDC), an estimated 4.4 million animal bites occur each year in the US. The annual incidence of dog and cat bites has been reported as 300 bites per 100,000 people. Most dog and cat bite wounds in young children occur on the face, head, and neck. By contrast, the extremities tend to be injured in young adults and adults.

Make sure everyone in your home wants a cat and will help take care of her.

members in your household. Does anyone suffer from cat-related allergies? Does everyone in the household like cats and want a pet cat? Do you have other pets in the house? How will they react to a new member of the family?

Who will take care of the cat on a daily basis? The cat will need fresh food and water every day. Who will buy the food and litter? Who will be responsible for keeping the litter box clean? Who will take the cat to the veterinarian when necessary?

Often, when a new pet is brought into a home, everyone volunteers to help out–at first. After a few weeks or months when the novelty has worn off, enthusiasm wanes. In some cases, what was once a positive, caring experience becomes a "chore" and the quality of the pet's care declines. Be sure everyone in the household understands the responsibilities involved in pet ownership and that everyone wants a cat.

Young children and cats should always be supervised when together.

Kittens look to you for extra love and care.

Cats and Children

The personalities and upbringing of any children in the household should be a deciding factor when choosing a pet for your home. You do not want the pet to hurt the child nor, obviously, the child to hurt the pet. Appropriate training and strict supervision is crucial in this process.

Cats and children can safely coexist in the same household as long as certain rules are followed. Small children need to be taught how to hold a cat properly, what not to do (such as pull the cat's tail or ears), and above all, to respect the cat as an individual being with feelings. (Cats are not stuffed animals and should not be treated as such.)

Children should be supervised whenever they are with the cat. Set a good example and show the child how to pet the cat, but also teach the child that sometimes kitty would like to be left alone and is not always interested in playing. Since both cats and young children are somewhat unpredictable, leaving them alone together is not a good idea until the child knows how to handle and respect a cat.

Respect is the main ingredient needed when raising children and cats together. You can help the process move along but, in reality, it is something that will just eventually "happen" between the two. If you are there to teach your child that a cat is not a stuffed animal to be handled roughly and treated carelessly, your child and the cat will get along fine.

It is difficult to state an exact age or time that a child can safely be left alone with a cat without your supervision. A lot depends on the maturity of the child and the personality of the cat. The longer you observe this child/animal bond, the safer everyone will be in the long run. If in doubt, separate the two when you are unable to supervise their interaction. This is one way you can be certain that both the child and the cat are safe.

Cats have been members of our society for thousands of years and are loyal, loving, comforting companions. Before making a cat or kitten a member of your family, take some time to consider all your options. Think about the type of cat you want to bring into your home and make a part of your life. Your new feline friend will quickly find a place in your heart and will provide you with a lifetime of love.

Cats are intelligent, loving pets that enrich the lives of their owners.

Kitten or Cat?

After deciding that you are going to take the plunge and find a feline friend, one of the most important decisions you will make is going to be the age of the cat you take into your home. There is a huge difference between adopting a vulnerable, active kitten and a mature, serene adult cat.

Kittens

There is probably no cuter sight to behold than a fluffy, adorable, two-month-old kitten frolicking and streaking through your house. However, this mischievous side to your precious baby will not only emerge when it is convenient for you. Kittens do not care about responsibility or timing. If she wants to jump on your head and claw your nose at two a.m.,

Kittens are curious, adorable bundles of energy.

Development of a Kitten's Senses

All kittens are born with baby blue eyes but they can't see a thing (or hear a thing) for approximately six weeks. Most cats' blue eyes, however, will gradually change colors over the first few months. Once kittens begin to hear, even as little tikes, their hearing is far superior to that of humans. They can differentiate the location of sounds, which will help them become exceptional hunters.

Your kitten will enjoy playing with you every day.

she will do it, no matter how you feel about it. You won't even be asked.

Owning a kitten is not a job to be taken lightly. Kittens are rambunctious. They are uncovering the joys that the world has to offer for the first time. Everything is brand new to them. What an amazing revelation when kitty finds out that the roll of toilet paper will go around and around and is perfect for shredding! And, of course, there are a million more treasures around your home just waiting to be encountered by your curious kitten.

The perfect age to acquire a kitten is after she has been weaned from her mother and can eat solid food on her own, usually after eight weeks of age. Taking a kitten away from her mother and siblings too early can result in an emotionally "handicapped" animal that may not have been taught essential behaviors, such as hunting or grooming.

Once the kitten has been taken away from her mother and littermates she may feel a little lonely and abandoned (after all, she's on her own now). This is one reason you need to step in and make the kitten feel like a loved and valued member of the household. Be sure to play with the kitten every day, several times a day. (If you adopted two kittens, this will be easy; they will constantly play together!) She will welcome the attention and you will be forming a bond with your new pet.

Having a kitten isn't all fun and games however. You are now responsible for the little life you've adopted and your kitten is depending on you for the best care possible. The

Kitten Safety

A kitten needs to be taught where she can and cannot go, for her own safety as well as your peace of mind. You don't want your kitten getting into places she can't get out of (such as a dresser drawer, or behind the refrigerator) nor do you want her climbing up the back of your sofa. Kittens are much like human toddlers; they can and will get into everything possible. Therefore, it is advisable to "kitten-proof" your home. The best way to do this is to think like the kitten. Get down on her level and crawl around on the floor to see what looks tempting. (It sounds a bit silly, but you'll notice the same things your kitten will.) Electrical cords, pen caps, rubber bands, household plants, and yarn or string make fun but dangerous toys for a kitten. Kittens will play with anything, and, all too often, they will try to eat their toys. All potential choking hazards need to be removed from the clutches of their tiny paws. Be sure you keep a close eye on your little bundle of fluff and watch out that she doesn't get into trouble exploring. Correct her with a gentle "No" if she goes somewhere or does something she shouldn't and redirect her attention on something positive.

first six months of a kitten's life are the most crucial for her overall health and well-being. Kittens are more susceptible and vulnerable to diseases and parasites during their first six months. Your kitten will need to see the veterinarian regularly for all the necessary immunizations that will keep her happy and disease-free.

Kittens also need to eat a special "kitten formula" diet. Most commercially manufactured brands of cat food have a type made especially for kittens. Be sure to find out what brand and type of food your kitten has been eating and stick with that brand while she's still in kittenhood. And, like any other pet, the kitten will need access to clean, fresh water at all times. It is a myth that kittens (or cats) "need" milk. Whole cow's milk may actually upset your little kitten's delicate stomach.

A young kitten may feel a little lonely when she's taken away from her littermates, so give her extra love.

Kittens should not be taken from their mother until they are at least 8 weeks of age.

Don't Start a Bad Habit

Although your kitten will need various types of toys to play with (the more toys the better, so kitty won't get bored), you should discourage her from playing with your hands or feet. When a kitten is a tiny, delicate creature, it is kind of cute to see her attacking your hand, which may be bigger than she is. But, as your kitten grows, her claws and teeth get bigger and sharper—and one day you will realize it is not cute when she attacks your hand.

The kitten (depending on what age you adopt her) may also need to be taught how to use the litter box. This shouldn't take too much time and usually once you show her the box and make a few scratching motions, she will understand what the box is for. Be patient with your kitten if she has an accident or two. Remember that she is still a "baby" and learning to function in the world around her.

Many people like to adopt a kitten so they can "watch her grow up" into a beautiful, adult cat and admire her changes and crazy antics over the years. However, a mature cat is equally capable of giving you the love and companionship you desire in a feline…and many adult cats are just hoping for a second chance.

Adult Cats

If you are thinking about getting a cat for your household, you might want to consider acquiring an adult feline. Most people want to have a little kitten around the house, but, as mentioned earlier, a lot of time must be invested in training a kitten.

The choice to adopt an adult cat, however, will mean not having to spend nearly as much time teaching the cat right from wrong. All it takes are a few short hours with an adult cat to find out her distinct personality and disposition.

In general, adult cats are more sedate and serene than kittens. They've had time to grow and learn and develop their own personalities. By the time the cat has reached adulthood, she should have learned basic "cat manners" and know what is expected (using the litter box) and what is not accepted in a household (such as scratching the furniture or jumping on the counter).

Adult cats are often more settled and serene than young kittens.

When you adopt an adult cat, you already know what you're getting. The cat will be full grown (or nearly so) so you'll know the size and weight of the cat you'll be caring for. After you spend some time with her, you'll also have a feel for her overall temperament, likes and dislikes. This isn't always true in the case of adopting an impressionable, active kitten. Adult cats are more settled and often make better companions to older people, or people with children, as they require less supervision, are not as wild and rowdy, and have acclimated to the world.

Adult cats are often overlooked at animal shelters because people want to adopt a cute kitten. This is unfortunate because most adult cats have known the

A mature cat makes a sedate companion pet and will welcome a second chance to live with people.

Find out as much as you can about the adult cat you wish to adopt.

Be Responsible

Although you may think you can control your adult cat's urges, you don't want to unwittingly contribute to the feline overpopulation problem. All responsible cat owners, especially in today's world of millions of unwanted cats in shelters, should have their pets spayed or neutered.

joys of living with a family before (for whatever reason) they were put up for adoption. A cat that has been given a second chance may bond more closely with a new human friend and will welcome the opportunity to be a part of a human household once again.

Although the mature cat has developed into a full-grown adult, she still must have certain needs met. Depending on the age of the adult cat you've taken into your home, you may have to get the cat spayed or neutered if the previous owner did not take on this responsibility. An adult cat should come to you with all her necessary vaccinations but will still need a checkup from the veterinarian. Adult cats can generally eat "regular" cat food, but some older cats may need a special food designed to prevent hairballs, or may be of the age to eat a "senior" diet. You will need to discuss the feeding requirements with your vet.

Talk to the owner (or breeder or animal shelter worker) and ask about the cat's history (or as much of it as is known). Your new cat won't be able to tell you where she came

Stop the Spraying Before it Starts

Have your male cat neutered as early as your veterinarian deems possible. Once your cat has started this marking habit, neutering may not stop him from continuing this behavior for the rest of his life.

Be sure to get your new pet spayed or neutered as soon as possible.

from or why she was put up for adoption. Sometimes cat owners give up their pets because they move, get married, or (sadly) because the novelty of having a cute kitten has worn off once the kitten becomes an adult. Some adult cats are given up for adoption because they have a personality or behavior problem, (not using the litter box, scratching the sofa) or they may not get along with other cats. Don't automatically rule out a cat with a problem, however, they can be just as loving and affectionate as any other cat. Find out as much as you can about the adult cat you want to adopt before you bring her home. This way, you'll have a good idea of what to expect from your new friend.

Of course, with the onset of adulthood comes sexual maturity for your cat. A cat will reach sexual maturity between six and twelve months of age and you need to be prepared. A female in heat will try to escape and look for a mate. A whole male cat (also known as a tom cat) may become aggressive and unruly upon reaching sexual maturity and will attempt to escape your home at every available opportunity. The male will begin a behavior known as "spraying" if you do not have him neutered. When a male cat sprays, he will back up against an object and urinate on it. This is a territorial behavior used to tell

An Advantage of Adopting an Adult Cat

Nighttime and post-litter-box kitty "craziness" are kept to a minimum in the older cat. If you have ever had a kitten, you must remember the nightly up-and-down the hallway or stairway madness that comes on at nightfall. The adult cat, when invited into your bed at night-will generally sleep, all but totally eliminating the early morning "in-your-face" attitude that kittens have when they want you to wake up. In short, the older cat is a delightful companion and you will probably end up getting a lot more sleep.

other cats that this is his domain. The odor from a male cat spraying is pungent. Most people cannot live with a male that sprays in their home.

Choose the Pet That's Right for You

If patience and time are not on your side, you may want to consider acquiring an adult cat that already knows how to use a litter box and knows what she should and should not use as a scratching post (the antique sofa that belonged to your great grandmother is a definite "No!"). Many people, unfortunately, take an irresistibly cute kitten into their home only to tire of her antics and get rid of kitty once she reaches that awkward adolescent age before becoming a full-grown feline.

Taking on the responsibility of raising a kitten and caring for her for the rest of her life–which could quite possibly be 20 years or more–is what you must consider before becoming a new kitten owner. It is not fair to this young creature to

Taking care of a kitten is a lifetime commitment.

discard her when she is no longer little and fluffy. You must think about the future of your pet before taking in an impressionable, helpless kitten. This is why an adult or older cat may be the answer for someone looking to adopt a feline.

Animals are not disposable. They are living, breathing beings and deserve the respect and love that is supposed to be a part of every life. Choose wisely (i.e. what is most reasonable and realistic for you to care for) between a kitten and a cat. It is a commitment you will need to honor for the rest of your feline's days.

Part 1

All cats deserve the chance to have a good home. Choose your pet with care.

Choosing the Right Feline for You

If you are actively searching for a cat, knowing how to choose the right one for your personal lifestyle is essential. Besides yourself, you should consider other family members, how active the household is, as well as other factors such as size (when full-grown), coat length, purebred or mix, gender, and temperament. Since you've probably already decided whether you want an adult cat or a bouncy baby kitten, there are a few other things to consider before making your final selection.

Pet or Show Cat?

The first thing you should consider is whether you want to purchase a purebred, or pedigreed, cat and compete in cat shows or whether you merely crave

Choose a cat that best suits your lifestyle.

Mixed breed cats make excellent family pets.

Genders of Cat Fanciers' Association's Top 25 Cats in 2001–2002

During the 2001-2002 season of the Cat Fanciers' Association's (CFA) cat shows, were the top 25 cats of that calendar year mostly male or did the female gender win more recognition? Out of the top 25 CFA cats, 17 of those were male cats while only 8 were females. In the top 10, 6 males made the grade while 4 females were included. The prize of Best Cat of the year, however, was awarded to a beautiful Copper-Eyed White Persian female.

a good friend and companion. While breeding is a legitimate business for most, some "backyard" breeders are only breeding these felines to make money off them by selling the kittens or perhaps winning money at a cat show. Buying a cat from a breeder will contribute to the vicious cycle of unwanted litters of kittens and cats that end up in shelters across the country. You must be very careful when adopting a cat from a breeder. You should get references from other customers who have adopted cats from this breeder.

Even if you do decide to purchase a purebred (with papers), the cat may not be show material because of behavior problems. Some cats like to "strut their stuff" in front of hundreds of people, while others might be too nervous to meet the demanding schedule and pressure of being a show cat.

Gender Decisions

Another point to be taken into consideration is the gender of the feline. This is a bit of a controversial topic; experts cannot seem to agree if gender actually makes a difference in the personality and behavior of a cat. The alteration of a feline obviously makes a behavioral difference in both genders because of the mating instincts it curbs, but is there a difference between the altered female and male?

Specialists in the field of animal science have studied virtually every movement, heartbeat, purr, and meow of the cat extensively, but there seems to be one area that hasn't received much consideration, the behavioral differences between the sexes.

Male cats will mark their territory by spraying, and this is quite unpleasant if done in the confines of your home. Neutering (especially if completed before the male reaches puberty) usually stops this behavior as well as territorial fighting with other males, roaming, and other aggressive behaviors.

Females left intact are unusually affectionate during their estrus cycle (also known as being "in heat"). This behavior includes rolling, rubbing, and other "overly-friendly" actions that are followed by continual yowling to attract a male. This more-than-cordial behavior is purely associated with "distress" and shouldn't be mistaken for adoration of you.

Many experts believe that after a cat has been altered, there is no difference in behavior between the sexes. Some people are convinced, however, that there is indeed a significant difference. In general, many male cats seem to be more affectionate and loving while females often are more aloof and standoffish. Again, it is important to point out that actual scientific evidence in the field of behavior patterns exhibited by already-altered cats is very difficult to find.

Although there does seem to be an overwhelming agreement that males are the best companion for affectionate cuddling and kissing, in no way does this mean males are necessarily "better" pets. Once you get to know and love your cat, personal preference must always outweigh any statistics or scientific studies.

Your cat, regardless of gender, will become a treasured member of your family.

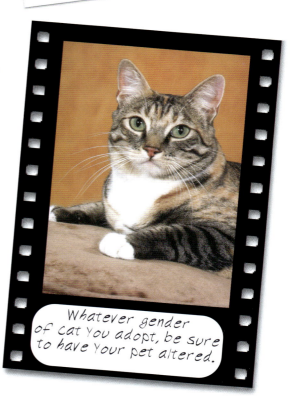

Whatever gender of cat you adopt, be sure to have your pet altered.

Part 1

If you decide you want a purebred cat, research the different breeds available.

Top Ten Most Popular Breeds

According to The Cat Fanciers' Association's (CFA) 2001 registration statistics, the top ten most popular breeds were:

1. Persian
2. Maine Coon
3. Exotic
4. Siamese
5. Abyssinian
6. Oriental
7. American Shorthair
8. Burmese
9. Birman
10. Tonkinese

Purebreds

Purchasing a purebred feline is not to be entered into lightly. You should definitely do your homework on all the different breeds available and find a reputable breeder (any of the cat registry associations, such as the Cat Fanciers' Association, can direct you in your search) to work with and find the right breed for you. Working with a purebred is not for everyone, however, and you may just want to find a loving, mixed breed cat or kitten in need of a good home.

Finding a reputable breeder–should you decide to buy a purebred feline–is important because you want to know your "investment" (and purebred cats are usually expensive enough to be considered as such) is healthy and well-socialized. This means kitty should have lineage papers, vaccinations (if possible) and have been handled by humans quite frequently during that critical socialization period of a cat's life. If you are not sure where to find a breeder, ask local veterinarians and/or area animal shelters. The Internet is also a good source of information when looking for a purebred cat.

Part 1

If you do decide to adopt a purebred cat, the personalities of certain breeds are pretty predictable according to the breed standards. Finding more information about such cats–like the CFA's top ten most popular breeds–can help you choose a cat who matches you and your lifestyle.

Persian

The Persian is, by far, the most recognized cat breed in the world and can be found in a variety of colors and patterns. Persians with color pointed patterns are Himalayans (in most feline registries). In Great Britain, the standard show cat Persian is more desirable with a moderate face type–termed the "doll face Persian" while in the US, the typical Persian is peke-faced. (This means that the cat will exhibit an extremely flat face, like that of a Pekingese dog.) Persians are normally docile, gentle, and loving felines, although at times they become quite playful…in their own way. This breed's long hair mats easily and daily grooming sessions are necessary to keep kitty in the best possible condition.

Maine Coon

The Maine Coon is known for its large size, easygoing temperament, and rugged appearance. This native New England breed is well-adapted to that harsh climate, with a heavy, shaggy coat, bushy tail, and tufted ears and toes. This breed has a lengthy, rectangular body with a square muzzle and is overall, a very sturdy cat. Despite the rumors, the Maine Coon cat is not a relative of the

Persians are the most popular purebred cat in the US.

The Maine Coon is a large, easygoing cat.

Part 1

The Siamese is a very intelligent, vocal breed of cat.

raccoon. The name only reflects the similarity of a Maine Coon's tail to that of a raccoon's tail.

Maine Coons can grow to be quite large. It is not unusual to find males who weigh over 20 pounds. Females are generally somewhat smaller than males, though noticeably larger than your "average" housecat.

Exotic

The Exotic has the body and head type of the Persian, but sports a short, plush coat. The breed was created by crossing Persians with other short-haired breeds. Generally speaking, the Exotic has a personality much like that of the Persian–compliant and gentle with a soft voice. They are usually lap cats and sometimes referred to as the "lazy man's Persian" because although the Exotic has the same body and head type as the Persian, the short coat means there is far less time spent on grooming.

Siamese

The Siamese is distinguished by its sparkling blue eyes and the colored points on the ears, face, tail, and feet that provide a prominent contrast to its light-colored body. Most people think of a "loud" cat when they ponder owning a Siamese, and they are right to think so. This breed is quite vocal, as well as sometimes demanding and should not be left alone for long periods of time. Boredom sets in quickly for this lively, intelligent cat. On the cat show circuit, today's Siamese exhibit a very elongated, thin body as well as a long, wedge-shaped head with extremely large ears.

Abyssinian

The Abyssinian is a very active, mischievous, and inquisitive feline. This slender, short-haired breed has a unique coat pattern that is ticked in the manner of a wild cat. Red (also known as sorrel) is the color most associated with this breed although they are also available in blue and fawn. Because of their high energy levels, many people think of an Abyssinian as a dog "stuck" in a cat's body.

Oriental

Orientals come in shorthair and longhair types. Oriental Shorthairs are like the Siamese in body type–long, fine-boned legs and tail, tubular body, wedge-shaped head, and large ears. Like the Siamese, the Oriental Shorthair is an outgoing, people-oriented breed. They are talkative, playful, acrobatic, and energetic. The Oriental Longhair is the semi-longhaired variety of the Oriental Shorthair. This cat also shares the slender body and active, people-oriented temperament of the Siamese.

American Shorthair

Developed from Native American working cats, the American Shorthair is a sweet, placid cat with, as its name suggests, a short coat. This was the first pedigreed breed recognized in the US. American Shorthairs are true workers–stocky, muscular, and powerful in build.

An Oriental Shorthair is a talkative, friendly cat, similar to the Siamese in body type.

Burmese

This breed is most likely an ancestor of the sacred brown cat raised by priests in the palaces and temples of ancient Burma (Myanmar, as it's known today). A Burmese cat is stocky and of medium size with good muscular development, short legs, and round feet. The head is extremely round with a short muzzle and wide, golden eyes. A Burmese cat's coat is short, fine, silky, and close.

Birman

This breed first appeared in Great Britain in 1919 and was called the Sacred Cat of Burma. A semi-longhaired, stocky cat with points, this cat is distinguished from other pointed cats by its four white feet. Birmans are quiet, passive cats with a strong love for their human owners.

The Birman is a large, semi-longhaired cat and is descended from sacred cats of Burma.

Part 1

This Tonkinese has a platinum mink pattern. Tonks are playful and affectionate to their owners.

Tonkinese

The Tonkinese, or "Tonk" for short, was originally produced by crossing a Burmese cat with a Siamese. This playful, friendly breed has a medium sized build with a soft, sleek coat. Tonks are unusual because many possess a unique pattern known as mink. While a Tonkinese sports points like the Siamese, the body is colored in a shade harmonizing with the point color and the cat has aqua eyes.

Mixed Breeds

There is a variety of names for cats that either don't have papers tracing back their lineage or whose parents (one or both) were not purebred. Alley cats, Moggies, non-pedigreed, mutt-cat, and mixed breed are just some of the terms used to refer to these felines who are not bred from any certain pedigree. But these are the cats most of us know—the stray and feral cats hiding in the cornfield across the road, or perhaps the faces staring at you from behind the bars at the hundreds of animal shelters across the country.

A cat doesn't need a family tree a mile long or a stack of official papers to prove her worth. Once you've experienced the deep and meaningful type of love that only a devoted pet can offer, you really won't care where your pet came from—only that she's with you, sharing the joys life has to offer.

Kiddie Compatible Kitties

Although most people end up adopting a mixed breed cat or kitten from a shelter or a friend, many cat lovers long to adopt a purebred feline with many of its behaviors already predetermined through breeding and genetics. Of course, cats cannot really be put into specific categories, but certain generalizations can be drawn among purebreds. Mixed breeds are hard to classify, so spending time with the cat and finding out its background is the best way to discover if a cat is kiddie-friendly.

The following breeds of cat are generally known for their compatibility with children (and this is just a small sampling), each individual feline will ultimately display her own unique personality.

Birman

Known as a feline who is extremely tolerant of children and other pets, the white-pawed Birman is a medium to large sized cat that can trace its roots back to Burma, where it was considered a sacred temple cat. The Birman is a smart and clever creature but does not loudly demand the absolute attention that some other breeds, such as the Siamese, solicit. Of course, to be tolerant of children, a cat must exhibit a patient and carefree disposition, which describes the Birman perfectly.

Burmese

The dog lovers will surely be charmed by the Burmese because they have many of the qualities that canine supporters love. They simply love people. Most cats will tolerate the human race, but loving them is an entirely different story! Large, innocent-looking eyes will almost mesmerize any unsuspecting human into granting this feline's every wish. But you will be generously rewarded as your Burmese wants to be by your side every second of the day. Whether "helping" you write a letter or keeping you warm under the covers at night, the Burmese is for you if you want a devoted dog in a cat's body.

Chartreux

This cat, which is commonly a muscular, solid adult, is a friendly, devoted feline and behaves somewhat like a dog when rough-housing with the kids or other

A Burmese can charm its owner with its mysterious and expressive golden eyes.

The Chartreux is a loyal, devoted family cat that loves children.

A Japanese Bobtail will enjoy a busy household and likes to be kept active.

The Maine Coon is a calm breed and is one of the most popular cats in the US.

household pets. The Chartreux is a very devoted cat and will remain loyal to you and your family throughout its lifetime. Its small, delicate voice will surprise you as you will expect nothing less than a lion's roar from such a robust cat. Although males and females both make excellent pets, Chartreux breeders normally agree that the altered male is the preferred choice among pet owners.

Japanese Bobtail

A great companion, the Japanese Bobtail (who can trace its roots back to Japan) is a delightful cat to have around anyone's home. The breed has a small pompom-like tail but no two tails are ever alike, thus each cat exhibits its uniqueness in its tail as well as in its personality. The Japanese Bobtail is in heaven when hanging out with its favorite humans. A friendly, intelligent feline, the Japanese Bobtail likes to be kept busy and active and adjusts well in practically any environment, including households with children and other pets.

Maine Coon

Before the Persian came onto the show circuit scene, the Maine Coon was the most popular among registered felines. After the long-haired, glorious Persian hit the US, the revered Maine Coon dropped into second place, and that is the spot it still holds today in the world's largest registry, the Cat Fanciers' Association (CFA). Maine Coons can grow to be some of the largest cats, yet are so gentle and easygoing that they are much sought after additions to any family. Despite the myth that this cat is part raccoon because of its fluffy, raccoon-like tail, there isn't much of a wild side to this good-natured and laid-back feline. It will readily adapt to most situations.

Solitude Loving Felines

If a cat breed is described as one that loves solitude, then it is safe to assume that boisterous, energetic children probably aren't included in any of the picture-perfect nine lives of these particular breeds. Again, cats can't be categorized, only generalized by what most felines of that breed prefer or how they behave. Here are just a few breeds that would most likely be happier without the presence of young children to disturb their peace and quiet.

American Shorthair

The American Shorthair is normally a quiet cat that doesn't require as much human attention as some of the other breeds. A home with children running around might not be the best environment for this particular cat. This is a cat who will be perfectly satisfied living in close quarters, such as an apartment or mobile home. Cats of this particular breed are called "gentle giants" because they are so even-tempered and loving–almost to the point of being shy. If there is someone at home most of the time, the American Shorthair will be perfectly happy with human companionship.

Contacting The Cat Fanciers' Association (CFA)

As the largest cat registry in the world, The Cat Fanciers' Association is a great place to begin your research on all the different breeds available—including their characteristics and behaviors. You can contact the CFA at:

The Cat Fanciers' Association, Inc.
1805 Atlantic Avenue
P.O. Box 1005
Manasquan NJ 08736-0805
Phone: (732) 528-9797
Fax: (732) 528-7391
Website: http://www.cfainc.org

The American Shorthair is descended from Native American cats.

A Korat prefers a calm, tranquil household and is best suited for homes without children.

Korat

The Korat is a rather rare find, which makes it all the more coveted amongst its proud owners. With origins in Thailand, the Korat is thought to bring Thai people good luck. This cat is very affectionate and loving and prefers a quiet evening at home. Although it is an energetic breed, the Korat does not like to be alarmed by loud noises and is easily startled. Because it is a quiet breed, the Korat is happiest in a tranquil environment.

Persian

The Persian is about as laid-back as a cat can be. Known for its sweet expression, the Persian's personality is built to match its pleasing looks. Persians are quiet and one of the more inactive breeds of cats, although they can be coaxed to play for short periods of time. Persians are loving and delightful felines to have around your home.

Ragdoll

As the name suggests, this is a breed of cat that loves to be held and just becomes a literal "ragdoll" in the arms of its possessor. A Ragdoll won't demand much of anything from its owner because it is one of the most quiet and gentle breeds around. This easygoing feline has a loving disposition and is not in the least bit aggressive. Much like the Persian, it is something of a showpiece that loves to be gently caressed and cuddled. The Ragdoll is almost a meek cat and prefers quiet and peaceful surroundings.

The long-haired Ragdoll loves to cuddle with its owners.

A Hairy Subject

Another factor to consider when deciding on a cat should be hair length. Some of the most stunning cats

Hairless Cats do Have Some Hair

Contrary to popular belief, there actually is no such thing as a completely hairless cat. Many people refer to the unusual-looking Sphynx as a hairless feline, but the fact is the Sphynx does indeed have hair. It consists of a very short, down-type coat that is close to the skin.

The Norwegian Forest Cat is one of the long-haired breeds available to cat owners.

are long-haired beauties, such as the majestic Persian. Persians, however, and other long-haired purebred or mixed-breed cats, require a lot of extra grooming care. Long-hairs will shed quite a lot and if white cat hair stuck on your black pantsuit isn't something you can occasionally handle, you should think about hair length in any prospective kitty.

Short-haired cats (or even those seemingly hairless breeds, like the Sphynx) are a lot easier to groom. All cats will shed a little bit so you will have to make friends with a good quality lint brush and your vacuum cleaner. If you have the time to brush and pamper a long-haired feline, then her beauty and grace is certainly worth the extra care. A short-haired cat, however, might be in your best interest if you want a

A Sphynx is not really a hairless cat. They have a short, down-like coat.

Cat Hair

Cats come in many shapes and sizes but the fur coat found on each feline is a big part of how they are classified. They usually fall somewhere in the categories of long-haired, short-haired, or "hairless."

Long-haired breeds include: Persian, Himalayan, Maine Coon, Norwegian Forest Cat, and Ragdoll.

Short-haired breeds include: American Shorthair, American Wirehair, Siamese, Burmese, Korat, and Singapura.

"Hairless" cats, such as the Sphynx, merely appear to be hairless. The breed actually does have a thin layer of hair covering its body.

low-maintenance cat in the grooming department.

Finding the Right Cat for You

Purebred or mixed, long-hair or short-hair, male or female–the ultimate decision of what cat is best for you is really within your heart. When you hold a certain cat or kitten and look deep into those mysterious eyes, what do you see staring back at you? If you can see a life of love and companionship in that reflection, you'll already know the choice has been made for you.

Where to Find Your Cat or Kitten

Once you have decided to get a cat and may have even made up your mind about what type of feline you are looking for (such as breed, gender, age, etc.), now the time has come to search for your perfect cat companion.

The Stray on Your Doorstep

Perhaps the most common way a person acquires a cat is one that does not include any special techniques or searching secrets: the cat finds you. There are many strays looking for some love and comfort from a family. Many strays were former household pets that, for one reason or another, were lost or dumped off by their original owners. It's a terrible tragedy when a housecat suddenly finds it has to fend for itself, so helping out that neighborhood stray is a very kind thing to do.

Sometimes a stray or abandoned cat will find you!

Part 1

Many stray cats started out as household pets but were abandoned or given away by their owners.

Overpopulation

In case you aren't aware of the ever-increasing feral cat population problem, consider this statistic: There are approximately 60 million domestic felines living in households across the country. Meanwhile, it is estimated that 60 to 100 million more innocent cats are out there on our streets, feral and homeless. We can all help fix the problem by getting every cat, feral or tame, homeless or owned, spayed or neutered.

Finding an abandoned stray sometimes almost seems like fate. After a careful examination by your veterinarian (including blood tests, necessary vaccinations, and making sure kitty is neutered or spayed), a homeless stray can become a very rewarding part of your family. Your new cat may be stressed out for awhile, worried that you will leave her, but an abundance of love and attention will soon put those fears to rest forever.

Often, you don't just find one lonely stray. It is very possible that you will find a stray mother with an entire litter of kittens. Irresponsible cat owners who do not spay their female felines may find it "easier" to dump off the pregnant mother cat somewhere instead of dealing with her and her litter. It is estimated that there are 60 to 100 million homeless felines in this country alone. Acquiring a cat or kitten by chance, instead of by choice, is something that happens more frequently than not.

There probably isn't a cat lover in the world who has not, at one time or another, taken a stray cat into his or her heart and home. It takes a hardened heart to turn away a lonely orphan facing another night on the streets or to ignore a starving kitty who desperately needs your help.

Feral Strays

There are two types of "stray" cats. A friendly stray is a cat who has had a home previously, while a feral stray is a wild feline who neither likes nor trusts humans (for a variety of reasons). With a lot of time and patience, you can get a feral cat to trust you, but a feral cat is not the ideal pet if you consider a pet something you can play with, cuddle, and shower affection on.

Feral cats have lived a hard life growing up without human contact (or maybe negative human contact). If a feral cat does come into your life, you can provide an outdoor shelter and food and water for your new cat companion, but probably will never enjoy the benefits of stroking the kitty on your lap while he or she sleeps away the afternoon. Make sure you live trap kitty and take him or her to the veterinarian for a checkup, but more importantly, have the cat spayed or neutered.

If you are fortunate enough to have a special connection with feral cats, you may find a lot of these kitties showing up in your yard as if a sign were out in front inviting them in. There are organizations that help people all across the country feed and care for entire colonies of feral cats.

Whether you come across a frightened feral or a sociable stray, helping out the homeless population of cats—one stray cat at a time—is an effort that will reap many benefits. The knowledge that you are doing something good by helping these orphaned felines will certainly enrich your life as well as the lives of the stray and feral cats you take into your heart.

Organizations Helping Feral Cats

To receive more information on helping feral cats, you can contact these national organizations:

Alley Cat Allies
1801 Belmont Road NW, Suite 201
Washington, DC 20009
Phone: (202) 667-3630
Fax: (202) 667-3640
Website: http://www.alleycat.org

Feral Cat Coalition
9528 Miramar Road
PMB 160
San Diego, CA 92126
Phone: (619) 497-1599
Website: http://www.feralcat.com

Friends and Neighbors with Cats to "Spare "

Being known as a "cat lover" sometimes has its pitfalls. Well-meaning friends and relatives automatically assume that, since you like cats, owning a few more is want you want. Many cat owners continue to let their females have litter after litter of kittens, not thinking about what will become of these kittens in a world already overpopulated with felines. Then these cat owners make the rounds of all their friends and family members to see onto whom they can "unload" the kittens.

Part 1

All kittens deserve good, loving homes.

You may find the perfect pet through a friend.

Suppose a friend or relative does call you and you are considering taking a kitten or two from him or her. It would be wise to have the kittens examined by a veterinarian, and then, before agreeing to take these kittens into your home, persuade the owner to agree that this litter will be their female cat's last litter. Specify that you will only take an animal from that person if they agree to spay their frequently pregnant mother cat. In this way, you have stopped a vicious cycle of kittens being born without a place to call home. You have the power to stop this cycle of pregnancies and unwanted kittens.

Normally, getting a cat from a friend or acquaintance is a safe bet because you will know what type of environment the kitten has lived in and the health and personality of the mother cat. You will also have had plenty of time to play with, hold, and pet each of the tiny furballs so you can make the best choice of which kitten (or kittens) in the litter was meant especially for you!

A Pet Store Kitten

Some (but not all) pet stores get their kittens from so-called "kitten mills." What this means is that cute, cuddly, kittens are produced as quickly as possible in an effort to make money. Often, the cats are being inbred and this frequently makes the pets coming out of these "mills" sickly or feeble.

It is to be hoped that laws will soon be enforced to stop these breeding-for-profit types of organizations. Please remember that not all pet stores participate in the "mill" form of purchasing their pets. You cannot automatically shun the notion of purchasing a kitten from a pet shop simply because of the mindset that all pet store kittens are from a "kitten mill."

The best way to find out what the practices are in the pet shop where you are considering purchasing a kitten or cat is simply to ask them and, more importantly, observe the animals. You can certainly tell a healthy, active, alert kitten from an unhealthy, sluggish, unfriendly one.

If you ask questions and take the time to observe the surroundings as well as the pets themselves, you will probably put to rest all of your doubts. If not, the best bet is to look elsewhere for a cat companion.

There are many advantages to adopting a homeless kitten.

Purchasing a Purebred Kitten from a Breeder

If you are not looking for the everyday, mixed breed cat, you will want to consult a breeder for a purebred feline. There are hundreds of breeders to choose from. Most breeders specialize in only one breed (occasionally you will find a breeder who breeds two or three types) and you will want to check out their credentials, such as what cat registry they belong to, etc. You can also get help with finding reputable breeders from such organizations as the Cat Fanciers' Association (CFA), the American Cat Fanciers' Association (ACFA), The International Cat Association (TICA), or one of the many other national or international registries. They can direct you to breeders in your area.

Purebred cat breeders will have a selection of kittens to choose from.

Kitten Free to Good Home

Searching through your local newspaper's classified advertisements is another way to find cats and kittens. In most cases, the felines are listed as "free to good home" and there probably won't be a price attached. Usually, the person placing the ad in the newspaper wants to get rid of a pet because he or she is moving or was surprised by an unexpected litter of kittens.

You should thoroughly check out the cat or kitten in question, however, and make a special note of the surroundings. Are they clean? Does the cat seem to be in good health? Be sure to get a history of the cat and ask questions. Will the person take the cat back if a veterinary exam shows that something is wrong? What vaccinations has the cat had? Be sure you feel comfortable with the cat and owner before you bring the pet home.

Ask around about the breeder or breeders you are considering buying your kitten or cat from. If you do not know anyone who has had dealings with this particular cattery, ask the cattery owners for a list of previous clients to see if the felines they adopted from this particular breeder turned out to be high-quality cats.

Although your phone book might have a listing for local cat breeders, the best place to find a reputable breeder could be at a cat show. Cat shows take place practically every weekend in cities all over the world. They will usually be sponsored by one of the hundreds of cat clubs and will be a CFA, TICA, or ACFA show–meaning the cats entered must meet the standards and criteria set up for the breeds in that particular registry (all registries have different rules and regulations). You can find out about upcoming cat shows in your area by looking in one of the several cat magazines available at most newsstands or checking with the individual registries themselves.

Obviously, breeders at a cat show will be showing cats that are registered. Many breeders place business cards on top of their cages for spectators and interested parties to take and use at a later date. A lot of breeders will be willing to discuss the breed in general and, more specifically, their cattery and the cats that they raise. You can learn a lot from these breeders. They are in the business of producing beautiful, high-quality animals.

Some breeders will also bring kittens from their cattery and have a "for sale" sign outside the cage. Don't make an impulsive decision and buy one right then and there. In any case, a breeder usually likes to get to know more about who will be taking one of his or her precious newborns home.

In fact, it is beneficial to both you and the breeder to learn more about each other before jumping into an agreement regarding a kitten or cat. Of course, you will want to know all there is about that specific breed before choosing your feline. The breeder will want to know about your intentions, as well, for the kitten. Will you be showing the cat? Using the cat to breed? Or will you simply be taking kitty home to love and cherish as a constant companion? All of these are suitable choices when buying a purebred.

Before buying your feline (or felines), make sure you've done your homework as thoroughly as possible. Be sure to visit the cattery where the kitten was born and raised. If a breeder is uncomfortable with your visiting the cattery, you should be cautious because there could be something the breeder is trying to hide-which is not a good sign.

Purchasing a pure-bred is a serious commitment. Ask the breeder to show you papers and medical records.

A breeder who lets you visit and spend some time at his or her cattery would be your best bet, although some breeders are extremely cautious when letting strangers into their facility due to the possible spread of germs. The cattery should look orderly and smell clean. The animals should be in clean, roomy cages or in a confined area. Males and females should not be allowed to run together as this could cause questionable breeding results.

All the cats should appear friendly and healthy. Signs of illness in any member of the group could spell trouble, as cats commonly pass diseases and illnesses to one another. You will want a breeder who actually spends time with the kittens and handles them daily. Early socialization with humans is crucial to a cat's overall personality. If you plan on showing your new purebred feline, you will need a sociable cat used to being handled by a multitude of people.

Cat Registry Organizations

There are many national (and some international) cat registries. If purchasing a purebred cat, the feline should be a member of a major registry organization. Here is contact information for a few of the cat registries:

The American Association of Cat Enthusiasts, Inc. (AACE)
P.O. Box 213
Pine Brook, NJ 07058
Phone: (973) 335-6717
Fax: (973) 334-5834
Website: http://www.aaceinc.org

The Cat Fanciers' Association, Inc. (CFA)
1805 Atlantic Avenue
P.O. Box 1005
Manasquan, NJ 08736-0805
Phone: (732) 528-9797
Fax: (732) 528-7391
Website: http://www.cfainc.org

Cat Fanciers' Federation, Inc. (CFF)
P.O. Box 661
Gratis, OH 45330
Phone: (937) 787-9009
Fax: (937) 787-4290
Website: http://www.cffinc.org

Fédération Internationale Féline (FIFe)
Penelope Bydlinski, General Secretary
Little Dene, Lenham Heath
Maidstone, Kent, ME17 2BS England
Phone: +44 1622 850913
Fax: +44 1622 850908
Website: http://www.fifeweb.org

The Governing Council of the Cat Fancy (GCCF)
4-6 Penel Orlieu
Bridgwater, Somerset TA6 3PG, UK
Phone: +44 (0)1278 427 575
Website: http://ourworld.compuserve.com/home-pages/GCCF_CATS

The International Cat Association (TICA)
P.O. Box 2684
Harlingen, TX 78551
Phone: (956) 428-8046
Fax: (956) 428-8047
Website: http://www.tica.org

Traditional and Classic Cat International (TCCI) (formerly known as TCA)
TCCI Secretary
10289 Vista Point Loop
Penn Valley, CA 95946
Website: http://www.tcainc.org

Look at the kitten's mother (and father, if possible) and try to imagine what the kitten will look like as an adult. Please note, however, that many breeders may pay someone in another cattery–with a suitable male–for "stud" service, so you may not be able to meet the father firsthand (although photos and papers should be made available to you).

Also, the behavior of the parents–especially the mother cat–is a sign of how your kitten will behave as an adult. Cautious, unfriendly parents often raise (or contribute to) cautious, unfriendly kittens. The entire feel and atmosphere is very important in your ultimate

Italian Government Makes Killing Homeless Animals Illegal

Did you know that in Italy, the government has taken it upon itself to help with the cat and dog overpopulation problem? In 1991, the Italian government passed a law making it illegal to kill homeless cats and dogs and also illegal to send them to laboratories for use in experiments. In the case of feral cats, Rome has adapted a policy by which feral cat finders can bring these homeless creatures to government-funded veterinarians for altering and vaccinations. The cats are then set free in the region they were found. To keep these animals from being captured more than once, a small, painless nick is taken out of the cat's ear during the time of the alteration surgery.

decision of whether or not to buy a kitten from the particular cattery in question. Trust your instincts.

A hefty pricetag is attached to many purebred cats and you'll surely want to get your money's worth and avoid getting an unhealthy cat or one who doesn't meet the required standards if you intend to show her at some point. Make sure you receive lineage papers and certificates as well as proof of inoculations and other important medical information.

Some people might question the logic behind owning a purebred kitten or cat when there are so many homeless, unwanted kittens in this world. However, if you want to become a serious cat show contender you may want to invest in a pedigreed cat.

Of course, showing your cat is not the only reason to purchase a purebred cat. When you adopt a feline from a breeder or cattery, you should know what you are getting before the kitten is even born. In fact,

Purebred cats possess certain breed traits. Research to see which breed is best for you.

Part 1

National Animal Shelters

Below is a list of some of the more well-known national animal shelters. Of course, there are thousands of local shelters overflowing with cats waiting to find homes. These national organizations can help you find shelters in your area:

The American Society for the Prevention of Cruelty to Animals (ASPCA)

424 E. 92nd Street

New York, NY 10128

Phone: (212) 876-7700

Website: http://www.aspca.org/site/PageServer

Best Friends Animal Sanctuary

5001 Angel Canyon Road

Kanab, UT 84741-5001

Phone: (435) 644-2001

Fax: (435) 644-2078

Website: http://bestfriends.com

The Humane Society of the United States (HSUS)

2100 L Street NW

Washington, D.C. 20037

Phone: (202) 452-1100

Website: http://www.hsus.org

North Shore Animal League (NSAL)

25 Davis Avenue

Port Washington, NY 11050

Phone: (516) 883-7575

Website: http://www.nsal.org

many breeders have every kitten already sold before the female (or Queen) has even been bred.

A kitten that is descended from a specific set of parents, grandparents, great-grandparents, etc., is almost certain to possess the qualities and personality that they are "expected" to possess. Although felines are very hard to label as individuals, generalizations are evident with each purebred kitten that is born into the cat world.

For instance, if you want a very vocal and possessive cat, without a lot of grooming troubles, you might consider a Siamese. Active and highly intelligent is the common personality for the Abyssinian, while a laid back, long-haired aristocratic type of kitty is normally what you can expect from owning the popular Persian.

Remember, you are not just investing money in this cat; you are also investing your time, your devotion, and your heart for the rest of your pet's days. Be sure that you make an informed decision for this lifetime commitment.

Adopting a Shelter or Rescue Cat

An animal shelter is probably the best place to look for a cat or kitten to adopt. By obtaining your pet from a shelter you are saving the life of an animal that might have no future. All shapes, sizes, breeds, and temperaments of cats and kittens are available at your local shelter. Although they all may look and act differently, all shelter cats have one thing in common—the need for a home to call their very own.

Animal shelters, rescue organizations, and humane societies have been around for many years. They provide food and shelter to needy and unwanted animals. Unfortunately, time, space, and money are limited, and as sad as it is, most of these unwanted animals are euthanized to make room for more of the same.

Over the last several years, steps have been taken to stop (or at least to lessen) the senseless killings of millions of homeless cats each year. Shelters and humane societies are coming up with alternatives by sponsoring no-cost or low-cost spay and neuter programs to try to keep down the exploding population of domestic animals. More pets spayed and neutered result in fewer kittens being born, thus fewer homeless animals in the shelters.

A new type of shelter has also arisen—the "no-kill" shelter. These animal shelters make it their mission to care for homeless animals for the rest of their lives and will not kill a cat simply because it has no place to call home. Of course, it takes lots of money and manpower

Kitten Adoption Fee: $40.00

Save a life and adopt from a shelter.

No matter where you obtain your kitten or cat from, be sure to give it lots of love.

There are millions of loving felines awaiting adoption.

to care for these homeless pets, so volunteers and donations are always in demand. Fundraising activities as well as generous donations from private individuals and corporate sponsors are helping these shelters stay afloat.

Please visit your local shelter before adopting a kitten or cat from any other source. There will surely be many choices and, if you choose to adopt from a shelter, you will know that your choice will help support an extremely important cause. At the same time, you will be making room for more cats to enter the shelter system and, with luck, find responsible, loving homes.

Unconditional Love

No matter where you get your cat from—be it a shelter, a breeder, or a neighborhood friend—every cat's needs are the same; food and water, a warm, dry shelter, quality health care and, quite possibly the most important ingredient of all—unconditional love from you.

Selecting a Healthy Cat or Kitten

So you've decided on the type of cat (or kitten) that you're looking to purchase or adopt. The next step is to choose a healthy kitty to welcome into your home. Getting a cat is a big responsibility, so be sure to do your homework and "shop around." Tell your friends and family members that you're looking for a cat and ask them if they can recommend a particular shelter or breeder. It doesn't matter if you obtain your feline friend from a breeder, rescue organization, or adopt a lonely stray—the bottom line is that the cat you adopt needs to be happy and healthy.

There are many important factors to consider when looking for a cat. Do your research ahead of time and bring a list of question to ask the person

A healthy, happy cat makes a great household companion.

Tugging at Your Heartstrings

When you are looking for a healthy cat, you may come across one that is "not quite right" for some reason. This cat may be ill, suffering from a medical or physical condition, or may be an aggressive or nervous type. Unfortunately, a cat like this is not a good candidate for adoption, especially for a first time cat owner. Although you may be tempted to take in and "reform" or "rescue" the cat because you feel sorry for it, avoid the temptation. Unless you have the time and patience (and in some cases finances) to devote to the cat, you may be getting in over your head. A cat with a chronic medical condition may need medication daily throughout her lifetime. Bringing a sick animal into your home could make other pets ill. New adoptees with personality disorders can upset the balance of the household if there are other pets present. If you adopt this "problem" cat and later find out that you cannot care for her properly, what will you do?

However, if you feel you have the time and energy to devote to a cat with special needs, then by all means take the cat home and give her all the love and care you can. But for the overall good of everyone involved, think the situation over carefully before making a final decision.

The cat you bring home should have a lively, alert appearance.

selling you the feline. You should know what healthy cats and kittens look like and act like and what the warning signs are of a potentially sick feline. Remember, all cats and kittens will seem adorable and try to capture your heart, but you need to choose one that is in the best of health so you can share a lifetime of happiness together.

A Healthy Cat Is...

It may sound simplistic, but a healthy cat or kitten looks healthy. Your potential pet should have a well-groomed, alert, clean appearance overall. Any kitten or cat that looks disheveled, unkept, or is trembling or unresponsive could be suffering from a variety of ailments. Be sure to examine any kitten or cat you want to buy or adopt before you bring her home. The following list will help you recognize a feline in good health.

The Coat and Skin

A kitten's or cat's coat should be clean, fluffy, and well-maintained. (This is particularly true of the long-haired breeds.) The feline's fur should be silky smooth and there should be no missing patches (which could be an indication of ringworm). Examine the cat and run your hands over the entire body, feeling for any lumps or hard spots. The cat's body should be smooth with no visible lumps. Be sure the cat is not overweight (a swollen belly can indicate worms), nor underweight (the ribs should not be protruding). The cat should have a solid feel to it overall.

Take a moment and check the cat for fleas. (This is easier to do on a white or light colored cat.) Look for small, black flecks the size of a grain of pepper. These are flea droppings and will usually be found at the base of the hairs around the chest and neck. Any feline can get fleas, and finding fleas is not a reason to avoid adopting a cat, but bear in mind that the cat will need to be given a veterinarian-approved flea treatment.

Cats wash themselves daily. The pet you adopt should look neat and well-groomed.

A Quick Test

One test to see how the cat or kitten moves is to stand a few feet away and call her to you. This will let you see how the cat walks (you'll notice any limping, stiffness in the joints, or balance problems) and will also give you an idea of how interested the cat is in you.

A kitten's coat should be clean, well-maintained, and smooth.

Make sure to examine your potential pet's eyes, ears, and nose.

How to Spot a Healthy Feline

√ Clear, bright eyes

√ Pink mouth and gums

√ Clean smelling ears

√ Silky, smooth coat

√ Appropriate weight for age

√ Active and alert to surroundings

Eyes

The cat's eyes should be clean, clear, and free of any runny discharge or tearing (which may indicate an illness such as an upper respiratory problem). Make sure the cat's eyes focus on you and are able to follow an object such as your finger or a piece of string moving in front of her.

Ears

Examine the ears. They should be clean and free from any waxy buildup. Dirty or smelly ears and a constant shaking or scratching of the head are often signs of ear mites. Ear mites are easily treated, and your vet can recommend an ear mite control product for your cat.

Mouth and Nose

Your cat won't want to say "Ah" so you can peer inside her mouth, but do it anyway. The inside of the mouth should be pink and smell clean (unless the cat has just eaten and has the dreaded "cat food breath"). Check the cat's teeth to make sure they are all intact. (Adult cats should have 30 teeth.) The gums should be pink and not swollen.

Check the ears-dirt or waxy buildup could be a sign of ear mites.

Part 1

An older cat's teeth may have some wear or yellow plaque buildup if regular dental care was not provided. A kitten's "baby" teeth (or milk teeth) should be white and bright and their mouths should appear pink and healthy. Milk teeth grow in at around two weeks of age. The kitten will lose her milk teeth somewhere between the ages of four and six months.

A cat's nose "leather" should be dry to the touch and there should be no discharge present. A cat that is not breathing through her nose may have a cold or other sickness.

Anal Area

The area around the anus and base of the tail should be clean and dry without signs of diarrhea. Keep in mind that some older cats or long-haired breeds may have problems cleaning themselves in this area.

A Checkup

If you are buying your cat or kitten from a breeder, he or she should provide you with proof of vaccinations and a medical checkup. Some animal shelters and clinics will do a veterinary exam, give the cat all necessary vaccinations, and, in some cases, even spay

Make sure the kitten or cat you adopt gets a veterinary checkup before you bring her home.

Quarantine

Until your cat gets a clean bill of health from the veterinarian, it is wise to quarantine the new pet from other pets in the household. You don't want to introduce any illnesses or diseases to your healthy pets.

Questions to Ask Yourself

When obtaining a cat or kitten from any source, ask a lot of questions. Don't be shy about asking anything that comes to mind. You are a customer and have the right to ask about the cat or kitten before your purchase it. The seller should be open and honest and be willing to let you look around at the cat's living conditions. Be suspicious if the seller seems evasive, can't (or doesn't seem willing to) answer your questions, or tries to pressure you into making a rush decision. Ask yourself the following questions:

√ Does the place you're obtaining the cat/kitten from appear clean? (How does it smell? Have the litter boxes been cleaned lately?)

√ Are other animals kept in appropriate housing? (How many cats are in one area or cage? Do they seem happy? Stressed? Are they in good health?)

√ Do all the cats and kittens have access to clean water, a litter box, and food? (If not, why?)

Trust your instincts. You should be able to get feel for a place that is less than respectable. If anything seems questionable, take your business elsewhere.

or neuter the feline before it is adopted out. Not all shelters will provide this care, so it is crucial that you take your new pet to the vet for a complete physical within the first 24 hours of purchase.

The veterinarian will give the cat all the inoculations she needs and do a routine exam. Your vet can find and treat any internal problems or illnesses not readily apparent to outside observation–such as worms or other parasites. Keep in mind that it is always a good idea for your vet to see your cat when she is healthy; that way the vet has an idea of what is "normal" for your feline and will have something to compare that against should your cat take ill.

Pick of the Litter

Suppose all the cats and kittens you see appear happy and healthy, how do you pick the "right" one? Often, a particular cat or kitten may catch your eye or decide to adopt you. But, if you can't decide right away, here are a few suggestions.

Look for a kitten or cat that seems interested in the activities going on around her. This shows that the feline has an interest in the outside or "human" world and will be drawn into the day-to-day actions around your home. Cats and kittens are curious creatures and should display an active, inquisitive nature. All cats and kittens deserve to be socialized and handled daily, whether they are coming from a shelter or breeder. This lets them get used to being around people, know what it feels like to be picked up and handled, and also promotes a trusting bond between the cat and humans. A well-socialized feline will not shy away from you, try to hide, or display any kind of fear behavior. Ask the person selling you the cat or kitten how often the feline has been handled.

Ask to see one kitten away from the rest of the litter and evaluate the kitten closely. See if you can develop a rapport or bond. Pick her up and pet her. Play with the kitten for a few minutes and see how she reacts to you. Kittens are used to being around their littermates and may act differently when alone (the shy kitten may play more, or the very active kitten may settle down and focus all her attention on you). Observe her–does she seem overly frightened when apart from her littermates? Calm and relaxed? Spend as much time as you need to with all the kittens until you find the one that is the best match.

An adult cat should display the same general qualities and have an interest in the surroundings, but most likely will not be as active as a basket of kittens. The older cat is more serene and may observe the setting in a more relaxed manner. Ask to see the adult cat out of her cage and take her to a separate, quiet room (if possible). Play with the cat and try to get a feel for her

If you like a kitten, ask to see her away from her littermates to get a feel for her personality.

Kittens and cats need handling on a daily basis. Cuddle with the pet you want to adopt.

An adult cat should be interested in the surroundings and curious about you.

overall personality. Pick her up and put her on your lap for some petting. Does she seem warm and friendly? Curious? Begin purring right away? These are signs that you've found a good match.

Choosing a pet is a big responsibility and one that cannot be taken lightly. Obtaining a healthy cat or kitten from the outset will lead to a longer, happier life for your cat. Make sure you take the time to examine all potential pets before you make a final decision. Don't rush out and get the first cute kitten you see–take the necessary time to ensure a good purchase–after all, you're investing in your cat's life.

Part Two

Caring for Your Cat

MPIFER © 2002

"Ball of string? Ball of STRING? I asked for a laptop!"

6

Before You Bring Your Cat Home

Have all the necessary supplies on hand before you bring your cat home.

The day has finally arrived–the day you will be bringing your new cat or kitten home. You know you are ready to see your new kitty experience all the wonders that her new surroundings have to offer–but is your house ready? Are you prepared?

Start with the Proper Supplies

The first thing you should do before kitty's arrival is to make sure you have the proper supplies on hand for your cat's basic needs. Your new pet will need a cat carrier or travel crate, food and water bowls, food, a bed, a litter box and scoop, litter, a scratching post, toys, a collar, and maybe even a leash.

Part 2

A sturdy cat carrier or crate is a must for transporting your cat home safely.

Be Prepared

Before you bring your new addition home, be sure to have the following on hand:

√ Cat carrier or crate (to transport your cat home in)

√ Litter box and scoop

√ Cat litter

√ Food and water bow s

√ Cat food

√ Brush and comb (for grooming)

√ Collar and ID tag

√ Toys

√ Scratching post

√ Cat bed

Cat Carrier or Crate

You will need to bring your cat home from the breeder or animal shelter in something safe and sturdy. A plastic cat-carrier or crate with a locking mechanism on the front will be secure enough for your cat–the Nylabone® Fold-Away Pet carrier is ideal! (A cardboard cat carrier or box is not sturdy and a frightened cat could easily escape or claw her way out.) The cat carrier should have adequate ventilation and allow you easy access to the cat. Be sure to get a cat carrier that will be large enough for your cat when she is full-grown. Put a towel or old sweatshirt on the bottom of the cat carrier so kitty has somewhere soft to sleep on the way home.

Food and Water Bowls

There are several kinds of food and water bowls available to pet owners. Some cat owners like to feed their pets out of stainless steel bowls. Steel bowls cannot become scratched or break easily, but some people question whether the food and water picks up a metallic taste. Other pet owners insist on using heavy earthenware or ceramic bowls for their cats. The bowls should be sturdy and bottom weighted so they cannot be tipped over.

(Use caution if you buy a painted ceramic bowl, some paint may contain lead that is harmful to your cat.) Plastic food dishes are not a good idea for pets. Over time the plastic can become scratched and germs and other bacteria can live inside the bowl. To prevent fighting over food, it is a good idea to have one food bowl per cat in the household.

Clean the food and water dishes daily and place them far from the litter box. (The kitchen is a good place for a feeding station.) Cats do not like to eat and eliminate in the same spot (and who can blame them?).

Find out what brand of cat food your cat likes to eat and stick with it.

Food

Be sure to have a supply of cat food on hand before your kitty comes home. Find out from the breeder or animal shelter what brand of food she's been eating and stick with it. Ask about food preferences. Does she like canned food as a treat? What flavors? Also find out if your cat has any special dietary needs. A kitten will need to eat a diet formulated for kittens, while an older cat might need a senior blend of food.

Cat Bed

A warm, soft bed will be a welcome sight to an exhausted cat. Although cats have a tendency to sleep wherever they are when they become tired, a cat bed will be a favorite spot to catnap. Cats feel safer if they can sleep in an elevated bed. If the bed or blanket is placed on a chair or sofa, you might have better luck getting kitty to sleep there.

Your new pet will welcome a soft cat bed in a quiet location.

Part 2

You can buy several commercially manufactured cat beds in pet stores. Make sure the bed is large enough for your cat to fit in comfortably, but small enough to give her a sense of security. Place the cat bed in a semi-dark, quiet, out of the way area of your home so kitty gets all the rest she needs.

Litter Box

A litter box will be the next item to obtain, and there are many different styles to choose from. If your new pet is a kitten, you will have to get a box small enough so the kitten can get in and out of it without any trouble. Otherwise, kitty may decide it's easier to eliminate elsewhere—which you do not want to happen.

If your feline is an adult (or when your kitten gets bigger), you will need to purchase a full-sized litter box. A lot of cat owners prefer a litter box with a hood on it. There are several advantages to this type, including privacy for your modest cat. Even more crucial is the fact that a hood or topper can prevent "overhang" accidents. An "overhang" accident occurs when a cat's feet are in the litter box but her behind is hanging outside of the box, thus allowing her to eliminate on your floor. This problem can be avoided by having a litter box with a hood.

Scratching Post

All cats need to scratch; it's part of their nature. When buying a scratching post, make sure it has a sturdy base and cannot tip over. Get one that is at least as tall as the cat is, so she can reach up to her full height and get the best stretch possible. There are a number of commercially made cat scratching posts available. Some have several different levels and perches, while other "kitty condos" allow the cat to play and nap on the top. If you have a large home, or more than one cat, get several scratching posts so kitty can scratch when she gets the urge.

Toys

Toys are a must for any cat owner. There are thousands of types of cat toys on the market, and each cat will have her

Provide your cat with a sturdy scratching post.

own favorite. Some cats like to chase ping-pong balls, while others like to pounce on catnip-filled mice. As a cat owner, your primary concern is to make sure that any toy you give to your cat is safe and does not contain any small parts that can be torn off and become choking hazards. Items such as small bells, feathers, pom-poms, etc. can easily be ripped off while your cat is playing with them. Do not give your cat rubber balls if the rubber can be chewed off and swallowed. In fact, do not give your cat any toy that is small enough to be swallowed. Play it safe and let your cat play safely.

Collar, ID Tag, and Leash (or Harness)

All pets should have a collar and identification tag with your name, address, and telephone number on it. Make sure you get a collar with a release that will prevent your cat from getting hung up on a tree branch if she goes

Be sure to give your kitten fun, safe toys. All cats love to play.

Feline Veterinarians

Should you take your cat to a "regular" veterinarian or one specifically in practice to treat felines? Many cat owners are turning to feline veterinarians, as they have more experience in treating cats and their ailments. Whatever type of vet you choose, make sure the vet's office is clean and neat, and the vet answers all your questions about your cat's health care.

RECEPTION
PLEASE CHECK IN

Some veterinarians treat cats only. All cats should have an annual checkup.

Part 2

Cats are naturally curious and like to examine everything. Be sure to "cat proof" your house.

outside. If you are going to train your cat to walk on a leash, buy a secure, escape-proof harness to go with it.

Cat Proofing Your Home

Everyone knows that when you bring a child into your house there are certain items that need to be put out of reach and other precautions to take so as not to injure the little tike. The same is true for your new cat. If you know how to prepare for kitty ahead of time, you will feel confident that the latest addition to your family will be safe, happy, and comfortable in her new environment.

It is best if you remember to treat your new feline as you would a human toddler entering your home for the first time. Accidents and mishaps do happen in places and at times you would never imagine possible. Cats can jump and climb, so even if you think something is out of reach, be sure to calculate if a jumper or climber could get to it.

Before your cat comes home, put away anything that could prove dangerous to your new pet. Creatures of extreme

High Rise Syndrome

There is an accident known as "High Rise Syndrome" that happens to many felines. Cats can sustain injuries from falling out of tall apartment building windows. Although cats usually survive a long fall, it is common sense never to leave a window open without a secure screen in it. Even if your cat does survive such a fall, she could have serious injuries.

How can a cat live after falling from a 15th floor window or patio? The secret is in the cat's amazing sense of balance. When the cat is falling, the fluid in the inner ear shifts and the cat rotates its head until it equalizes and the fluid is level. Kitty's body automatically shifts to follow the head, and the cat lands on her feet. A cat is extremely agile, and her fluid muscles respond instantly. A cat has 30 vertebrae—5 more than humans, which accounts in part for this amazing agility.

The Cat's Remarkable Jumping Ability

Have you ever wondered why, when you put a feline in a big box or put up a tall fence that you just know she can't hurdle, your cat always manages to surprise you? Cats are magnificent jumpers and most are capable of jumping five times their body length. A twenty-inch long kitty could qualify for an amazing five-foot jump when trying out for the Olympics.

Cats are excellent jumpers and often go places they shouldn't.

curiosity, cats will eventually examine every nook and cranny of your home. Be sure that anything toxic is put away in a safe location. Don't forget that many cats learn how to open cupboards and pantry doors. Nothing can be considered safe if you think of kitty as a toddler–medicines, cleaning supplies, sharp objects, etc. must all be out of reach for your new and extremely curious companion.

Everyday household items can be dangerous to your cat. Simple things such as lit candles, cleaning products, plastic grocery store bags, rubber bands, and pen tops, can all cause harm to your cat or kitten. To be on the safe side, bend down and take an inventory from your cat's point of view. Do you find potential choking hazards such as paper clips or bits of string under the sofa?

Cats and Houseplants
Many homeowners believe that healthy greenery helps make their house a home. As much as you love your plants, is it safe to have plants and cats? Besides the fact that many cats find your houseplants fascinating merely because there is dirt in them (perfect for using as a litter box at any given moment) many houseplants are actually toxic to cats. The best way to play it safe is to rid your house of all poisonous plants. Even if you think you

Some plants found in and around your home are poisonous to cats.

A Trip to the Vet

Before you bring your new cat home, take her to the vet for a checkup. The vet will be able to get an idea of her overall health and make sure she has all the vaccinations she needs to start a healthy life in your home.

can keep your plant away from your cat (by hanging the plant from the ceiling, for instance) your persistent, acrobatic cat just might find a way to make it up to the plant and the results could be deadly.

Beware of Toxic Plants

As a responsible pet owner, you need to be aware of the numerous plants that can be poisonous to felines. According to the American Society for the Prevention of Cruelty to Animals (ASPCA), some houseplants can be quite harmful if ingested by an animal.

The ingestion of azalea, oleander, castor bean, sago palm, Easter Lily, or yew plant can be fatal. Chewing on some plants may result in severe irritation to the mouth and throat. Other plants, while not quite so deadly, may cause a severe intestinal upset. You should know the names of all your plants and keep any potentially toxic plants out of areas accessible to your animal companions.

If your cat ingests a poisonous plant, you must contact your veterinarian immediately. You can also call the ASPCA National Animal Poison Control Center for 24-hour emergency information at (888) 426-4435. Please note that in order to provide top-quality medical assistance, there is a consultation fee for this service.

Some Of The More "Popular" Plants Toxic To Cats

Although there are many plants that can prove toxic to your cat, this short list is just a few of the more well-known – or popular – plants that are often found in the homes of plant enthusiasts.

Aloe Vera	Iris
Amaryllis	Marigold
Azalea	Mistletoe
Baby's Breath	Morning Glory
Bittersweet	Oriental Lily *
Bleeding Heart	Peony
Bluebonnet	Periwinkle
Chrysanthemum	Poinsettia
Daffodil	Primrose
Easter Lily *	Rhododendron
Eggplant	Rubber Plant
English Ivy	Schefflera
Eucalyptus	Tiger Lily *
Ferns	Tulip
Geranium	Wisteria
Heartland Philodendron	*Lilies are especially dangerous to cats and should be avoided at all costs!
Holly	
Honeysuckle	

Playing with Your Houseplants

Okay, you checked and re-checked until you are certain that every piece of greenery in your home is safe for your cat to eat. Of course, that doesn't necessarily mean you want your cat to eat your beloved plants, nor do you want her to use them as toys, or worse. It is important to set boundaries that your cat can understand. Some greenery belongs to you

Your curious kitten should be taught to stay out of your plants.

Cats and Grass

Most cat owners have witnessed, at one time or another, an unwell feline snacking on outdoor grass. This seems to have a medicinal purpose for them. Experts know that grass can cause a cat to vomit, which helps bring up excess fur that's been swallowed.

Some cat owners will pick grass from their lawn (make sure that no lawn chemicals have been added to kill weeds) and bring it inside for kitty to graze upon at her leisure.

You can also buy a special kit of "cat grass" at your local pet shop or in most grocery stores. The kit comes with seeds of grass that are safe for your cat to eat. This is one way of bringing the outdoors indoors for your feline friend. Whether planted and grown in a kitty container, or plucked from a chemical-free lawn, providing greenery to supplement her diet is a generous gesture your cat will surely appreciate.

(such as your houseplants), while other greenery is meant especially for your cat. You need to establish these boundaries right away. Encourage kitty to nibble on grasses meant for her and consistently discourage her nibbling and playing with your plants. Hanging plants from ceiling hooks, or keeping them in other out-of-kitty-reach locations (such as on high bookcases or shelves), is the most acceptable form of discouragement. A quick squirt of water from a spray bottle (along with a stern "No!") can also be a sufficient deterrent.

Having a house filled with the breathtaking scene of nature at its finest—plants, greenery, and other foliage—does not have to mean a lifelong struggle with your furry friend. If you provide your cat with her own edible greenery, then filling your home with non-toxic houseplants shouldn't be a cause for concern. And, in the unfortunate case that your curious, acrobatic cat does find herself hanging from the ceiling while chewing on your most-prized plant, at least you'll know her supposedly inaccessible snack won't be deadly.

Don't Let Your Feline Get Burned

Often, a person's vision of the ideal home atmosphere includes an overstuffed easy chair placed beside an inviting fireplace with a contented cat curled up on a plush rug. Portraits of fireplaces and felines together are quite common because it is a comforting vision of warmth, coziness, and "home" all wrapped up into one perfect image. This ideal could never be compromised by kitty suffering a burn from the tranquil fire, right?

Cats, like humans, can and do get burned, either from getting too close to the fire in a fireplace or from a flying spark. To protect your cat, as well as any pet, the first rule to remember is never to leave kitty unsupervised with a fire burning or smoldering. There are many ways to prevent your cat from coming in direct contact with the flames, such as a fireplace screen. Screens can be opened, however, and what you think could never happen might become a harsh reality.

Cats have a tendency to seek out warm places. Since kitty's normal body temperature of between 101 and 102 degrees is somewhat higher than the 98.6 degrees standard temperature for humans, seeking out the warmth from a fireplace doesn't seem that unusual. Some cats are very afraid of fireplaces–which is probably a good thing because it lessens the risk of injury. Other cats, however, have been known to practically stick their noses into the open flame or get their tail too close for comfort.

The ever-popular phrase, "curiosity killed the cat," certainly has some meaning behind it. Felines can get into anything, and even if they've never done such a thing before, there will always be a first time. Total supervision is necessary while you have a fire burning. Keep kitty in a separate room (with water, food, and the litter box, of course) if necessary. This rule doesn't just apply to fireplaces, of course, but to anything that could burn your cat, including your stove, an iron, lit candles, or a grill.

If Kitty Gets Burned

Would you know what to do if your feline friend caught fire or was singed by a loose spark? Basically, you would do the same thing you would do for a human on fire–roll her. If you are near the cat, grab her and roll her on the floor–preferably wrapped up in a towel or rug–to extinguish the fire.

If You take all the necessary precautions, Your cat will be happy in Your home.

Do not panic or kitty will run and hide. If your cat gets injured by any type of burn, you should have her examined by a vet—just to be on the safe side.

A Safe Home is a Happy Home

A safe household is a happy household. There are obvious dangers and, of course, not-so-obvious dangers, all around your house. It is your job to safeguard any pet that enters your home. However, if you thoroughly prepare your house before your furry friend arrives, you will be able to relax and enjoy the newest addition to your family without any worries. And remember, your home is now your cat's home, too, so be willing to share it with her to the fullest extent.

Settling In—
The First Few Days

Your feline's first days in her new home can be exciting and yet intimidating. Although you will be thrilled the day you bring home your new family friend, keep in mind that your kitten or cat will need time to adjust to her new surroundings. Remember that your house, family members, and other pets all seem strange to her. Be patient with your cat for the first few weeks until she becomes used to living in her new home.

What to Expect

Everyone is excited when a new kitten or cat is brought into the home. It's an important day for everyone, both human and feline. Friends and family members will want to come over to see and play with the new, adorable kitten. Your children may want to

Everyone is delighted to have a new cat in the house.

Part 2

Your cat will be nervous and flighty until she settles into your home.

Prepare a separate area for your new kitten until she adjusts to her surroundings.

hold and cuddle with the new cat. However, at this time, you need to provide your kitten or cat with just the opposite, if only temporarily.

Your new arrival will most likely be afraid and stressed out when you bring her home. After all, if she's a kitten, she's just left the only world she knew behind. You are a stranger to her and she may seem a bit shy or nervous at first. Your kitten will miss her littermates and may cry for her mother, so you must be patient, loving, and soothe away her fears. She won't know what to expect in this new place and may be startled by anything loud and different (like a vacuum cleaner or the television). An adult cat may have lived in another house and will know what to expect from life with humans, but all of the familiar signs and smells of what used to be "home" are gone. Do all you can to make your cat or kitten feel as comfortable and secure as possible until she has settled in.

You should prepare one room (such as a spare bedroom or bathroom) where your cat can spend her first day or two. Provide kitty with a soft, warm cat bed, toys, a litter box, food and water. Let her live in this special room until she has adjusted to being on her own. A quiet, safe place will help your cat settle into her new home faster. Make your cat as comfortable as possible and keep visits by well-meaning friends to a minimum. Talk to your cat calmly as you pet and play with her.

After your cat has adjusted to life in her special room, you can let her explore the other parts of the house (after they've been cat and kitten proofed, of course). It's a good idea to start out slowly. Let your kitten explore one or two rooms a day until she feels comfortable, then allow her into other parts of the house as she relaxes in her new environment.

Preparing Your Family

If you've never had a cat before, you will need to make sure your family knows what to expect when you bring home your new pet. Although small children will be curious about the kitten or cat, they should not be left alone with the pet for any length of time. The child may accidentally do something (such as pull on the tail) to cause the cat to scratch or bite. Older children who have been taught to

Teach your family members the correct way to hold a cat.

Holding

Teach your family members the proper way to hold a cat. Hold the cat under the chest and support her feet with your arm or hand so her legs do not hang free. This will give kitty a feeling of comfort and stability.

Part 2

Other cats in the house may display aggression to the newcomer.

Other Pets

Introduce the newcomer to any other household pets before you allow her to explore freely. You can use a crate or cat carrier to let the cats see and sniff each other (the crate will keep them from fighting), or allow them to meet "nose to nose" under a closed door. Cats are territorial, and more than likely, the established cat might not take kindly to a new kitten scampering around. Be aware that the cats may fight, hiss, or growl at each other until they learn to get along. Never leave two cats together until you are certain they will not fight.

respect the cat can help kitty adjust to life in the new home by playing with her and helping out during feeding time. This not only benefits the cat but also lets the child know what is required to take care of his or her new feline friend.

Family members will need to learn a few "rules" for cohabitating with a cat. Doors and windows cannot be left open or ajar, otherwise the cat may escape. If a small kitten is in the home, be sure she cannot fit behind appliances and get stuck, or crawl under, or into, any reclining chair. Children should be instructed not to play roughly with the cat and not to pull on the ears, tail, or whiskers. Everyone should remember not to leave small objects, such as rubber bands, paper clips, or buttons where kitty could find them and accidentally swallow them.

Your new arrival will have a lot to learn when she moves in. In addition to learning where the litter box is, what time she can expect to be fed, and where to find the best bird-watching spot, she will have to learn "rules" of the household. Teach your cat or kitten what is and isn't acceptable in your home. Show her where the scratching post is so she won't claw the sofa, instruct her to stay off the counter, but do allow her to jump onto a favorite windowsill or cat perch.

Spend some quiet time getting to know your new cat.

Your cat will feel at home in no time at all.

Part 2

Introduce your cat to her new home slowly and with patience. In time, you will learn all about your feline's personality, her likes, and her dislikes. Spend quiet time getting to know each other. The first few days you spend with your cat may be the most important ones, as these are the days where your tiny kitten or cat learns to trust you and see you as her new friend and protector.

Feeding Your Cat

Feeding your cat the correct diet is something that every cat owner should think about at every stage in kitty's life. What you feed your kitten is not what you will (or should) feed her when she becomes an adult cat and then a senior. Each stage of life demands different nutritional requirements; you need to know what these dietary needs are and when they should change.

Kitten Nutrition

Many people still believe that giving a kitten a bowl of warm milk is just what she needs to lap up before taking a long nap. However, cow's milk is the last thing your kitty should have for a meal, as most felines are lactose-intolerant. Although they may greedily lap up any cow's milk that you offer them,

Your cat will become accustomed to the feeding schedule and expect to be fed on time.

Despite the myth, cats should not be fed bowls of milk. Most felines cannot digest it.

The Milk Myth

As hard as it is to believe, most cats are lactose-intolerant and cannot properly digest milk. When you visualize a contented cat, that picture often includes a cat drinking from a saucer of milk. Although felines can drink their mother's milk, the milk that humans normally consume is something that not should be given to any cat – no matter what her age.

they can't properly digest it, which may lead to a bout with diarrhea. Diarrhea in a small kitten can quickly lead to dehydration and, in the worst-case scenario, death. It's best to avoid giving your kitten any cow's milk–no matter how much kitty seems to love it!

Orphaned kittens that haven't been properly weaned from their mother's milk can be bottle fed a milk replacement supplement that you can get either from your veterinarian or in a pet supply store. You can try to get the kitten to drink the milk replacement from a shallow bowl but, until she does, a sterilized baby bottle will have to do.

When kittens do start to eat solid foods, you should consult with your veterinarian about the best type of food for your particular kitten's needs. Generally speaking, most pet food manufacturers make kitten formulas in dry, semi-moist, and canned food for

An orphaned kitten, or one who has not been weaned, may need to be bottle fed.

optimal health. As long as your veterinarian approves your choice in kitten food as complete and nutritious, you can feel safe in knowing your kitten will grow into a healthy adult.

Adult Cat Nutrition

Once your cat has matured into an active adult feline, the food you fed her as a growing kitten needs to be changed into something more appropriate. Since kittens grow at an accelerated rate, a kitten diet is more concentrated than food meant for adult felines. After kitty reaches one year of age, she can be considered an adult in terms of feeding. If you continue to feed kitten food to an adult cat there is a real danger of your adult cat becoming overweight.

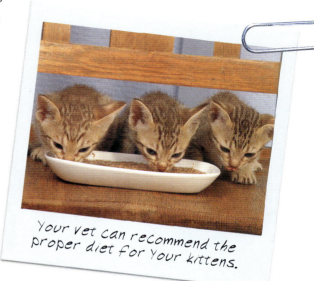

Your vet can recommend the proper diet for your kittens.

An adult cat can be fed a commercially made cat food specifically manufactured for the adult cat. Your veterinarian can help you pick out the right cat food for your cat's special needs (if any) or recommend a nutritionally-balanced diet for the adult cat. Of course, you have many choices when shopping for cat food–from generic to brand name to premium. Generic food should probably not be what you feed your cat because it often doesn't have the essential nutrients to sustain a healthy adult feline. Premium brands of cat food (which you can get from your veterinarian) or brand names (such as those sold in pet stores and grocery/department stores) will usually be fine for a full-grown cat.

Necessary Nutritional Requirements

Not all commercially manufactured cat food is

Taurine

One ingredient that all cat foods should have is an essential amino acid called taurine. Cats who do not get enough taurine in their diets can suffer severe eye problems, possibly leading to blindness. The latest studies have shown that taurine also prevents heart disease in felines. One interesting note is the fact that canines do not need any taurine, so, as most cat owners should already know, cats should not be allowed to eat dog food. It doesn't contain that feline-necessary protein, taurine, or at least not the amount a cat requires.

Cats as Carnivores

As true carnivores, cats need a diet of approximately thirty percent protein. Foods high in saturated fats are essential for proper hormone production. The extra protein is vital for a cat's specific amino acid, vitamin, and mineral requirements. Cats make extremely efficient carnivores because, while they can metabolize some plants with nutrients, they can absorb vitamin A only from meat.

Cats love the outdoors. Occasional walks (on a halter and leash) will keep them fit.

the same. Some "premium" brands may contain more of the necessary vitamins and minerals your cat needs to stay healthy as compared to a cheaper, generic brand. Overall, adult cats need a diet containing about 25-30 percent protein and 10 percent fat. Vitamins are essential to a cat's diet and are found in most commercially prepared cat foods. Do not give your cat any vitamin supplements unless specifically prescribed by the veterinarian. An excess of vitamins can be dangerous to your cat.

Senior Cat Nutrition

Many cats have special dietary needs, but none more than the elderly cat. If tooth care has not been a priority in the younger cat's life, perhaps dental disease has softened kitty's teeth so much that she can't chew the dry, crunchy foods she once did. This is certainly something to consider when choosing the senior cat's type of food. If she can't handle dry food, you may have to put her on a diet of moist and semi-moist food, which is softer to chew.

It may appear that your older cat isn't eating as much as she used to. This is probably true because the senior feline isn't nearly as active as the once-frisky kitten or mobile adult cat. Once a cat's activity level begins to wane, she won't need as much energy (food) to sustain herself on a day-to-day basis. In fact, most of her time will be spent sleeping (if it is indeed possible to sleep any more than an adult cat or kitten already sleeps!).

Finally, as with the other stages of kitty's life thus far, pet food manufacturers make special formulas for the senior cat. These foods will have "For Senior Cats" listed somewhere on the bag or box. Senior food won't be difficult

Part 2

to find because almost all the pet food companies are recognizing that our felines are living longer and need specific food for the later years of their lives. Your veterinarian will always be able to recommend what your elderly cat needs in her diet to live out the rest of her years as healthy and as happy as possible. A healthy diet prolongs a cat's life.

A senior cat generally needs fewer calories than a more active, younger cat or kitten. As your cat ages and becomes more sedentary, cut back on the amount of calories you feed her so she does not become overweight. Carrying around excess pounds can be a strain on an older cat's system. Your vet may recommend a low-calorie senior blend of cat food for your feline.

So Many Cat Food Choices, So Little Time

When you have a cat, many questions arise regarding what brand of food to feed her, how often, when, where, how much, and even what consistency–dry or wet–will be best for her. Of course, the food has to taste good, be nutritious, and be affordable. Although all these questions seem confusing and it can appear to be a lot to learn, once you get the hang of feeding your cat the right foods at the right time in the right amounts, it will become second nature to you.

Dry and/or Wet Food

There are numerous versions of dry and wet cat food available. Many experts recommend combining the two for a mixed meal or alternating between the two. Dry food is good for a cat to eat because it helps promote healthy gums and teeth. Wet, canned cat food seems to be more of a treat for kitty and is not recommended as the only food to feed your feline. Always read the labels

Do Cats Chew Their Food?

Sometimes you may think you hear your cat chewing her food. In reality, cats do not chew, but instead, chop their food with their sharp teeth and swallow it relatively whole.

Can Cats be Vegetarians?

Cats cannot survive on a vegetarian diet. In 1982, taurine, an amino acid only present in meat, was found to be crucial for the healthy functioning of the cat. Taurine is vital for aspects of metabolism, eyesight, cardiac function, bile formation, and reproduction. Cats are not able to produce sufficient taurine themselves and must have an adequate dietary supply. Since taurine occurs almost solely in materials of animal origin, cats should not be fed on a purely vegetarian diet.

Part 2

Your cat may enjoy an occasional treat of wet or canned food.

on your cat food bags and cans to make sure the food is full of nutrients instead of empty calorie fillers. Also keep in mind that cats get much of their daily liquid requirements from canned food because water actually makes up a significant portion of most canned cat foods' content.

If you cannot choose a cat food, your veterinarian will be glad to pick out the perfect type for your cat's particular age and activity level. Today's choices are wide and varied, with flavors ranging from roast beef to flaked tuna. There are special foods for cats with weight problems, urinary tract problems, hairball problems, and a host of other feline concerns.

Free Feeding Versus Scheduled Feeding

There are two options when considering the feeding of your cat. Some people prefer to leave food out 24 hours a day so their cat can nibble any time she feels hungry. This method avoids the 3:00 a.m. "Wake-up-I'm-hungry!" calls from a famished feline. Other people, however, fear their cats will become overweight if allowed free access to food all the time so they feed their cats on a schedule. Beware, however, if you are ten minutes late on the schedule. Whether you believe it or not, cats can tell time.

A Variety of Bowls to Choose From

You should note that there is a difference between the types of food and water bowls you can provide for your feline. Plastic bowls are not recommended because they often get bacteria in the cracks and crevices and they can make your cat sick. Steel bowls are safe and can be thoroughly cleaned, but you may wonder about the "taste factor" (i.e. why don't humans eat or drink from steel plates and glasses?).

If you leave food down all day, your cat can eat whenever she is hungry.

Taste-Testing Felines

Did you know that when your cat takes a drink of something, she usually doesn't swallow any of the liquid until after four or five practice laps? It seems that kitty is testing things such as the temperature and quality of the beverage she is about to drink before taking the actual plunge.

Whatever type of food bowl you use, be sure to keep it clean at all times.

Heavy glass is the best type of bowl to use for your cat because it cannot get broken easily (as long as it's kept on the floor) and cleans up nicely. Ceramic bowls sometimes contain toxic leads and should be avoided if you're not sure what materials are used in the paint.

Cleanliness is imperative because old or spoiled food in a dish will certainly turn kitty's stomach and cause her to avoid the food bowl. Of course, keeping any type of bowl extremely clean (but without soap or bleach residue) is probably one of the most important parts of the feeding and watering process.

Finally, no matter what age or size your kitten or cat is, fresh, cool water should be available at all times. Even if it appears your cat is not drinking any water, it should still be available because you may not see the kitten take a few drinks every now and then.

Water is an essential part of any animal's diet. If you are not sure about the taste or chemicals in your tap water, bottled natural spring water (which can be found at any grocery store, department store, or convenience store) is recommended.

Battling with a Finicky Feline

Everyone remembers the television commercials featuring America's most "finicky" cat,

If your feline stops eating, she may be upset over a change in her diet, or may not be feeling well.

Do Felines Have a Sweet Tooth?

If you've ever offered your dog a cookie, you know it will be gobbled up in an instant. The same is not true, however, with your cat. The reason? A cat does not have taste buds that will detect sweetness; therefore it can't be tempted with sweet rewards. Those finicky felines can, nevertheless, discern the slightest peculiarities in different waters.

Morris. Giving him a certain brand of cat food changed everything and he was finicky no more. If your cat won't eat, the first thing you should find out is if kitty is ill. Sick felines do not have much of an appetite and your cat's finicky palate could be the first clue that something is not right with your cat. If your cat suddenly develops a finicky disposition, the veterinarian's office should be your initial stop in correcting the problem.

If everything checks out okay at the veterinarian's office, then you should consider some common reasons why cats sometimes are (or turn) finicky and try to solve the dilemma. Believe it or not, your cat isn't going to starve herself (no matter what impression she might be giving you). In fact, cats can go several days without eating. Before cats were domesticated, they had to kill their own prey and it was not uncommon for them to go a day or two without eating. Anything longer than a few days, however, is not normal. Keep in mind that they must continue drinking fresh, cool water every day.

Changes in Diet

Another reason your cat may decide to become "finicky" and refuse to eat her food is that you've switched cat food brands or flavors recently. Most cats are very routine-oriented and

Could Your Cat Possibly be Spoiled Rotten?

This is a hard one for any pet owner to admit, but maybe your cat isn't really all that finicky. Instead, maybe she is just spoiled rotten! Maybe she is so good at getting her own way that she can have you cooking up an entire fish entrée with one sad look at her food bowl.

Your cat isn't finicky. You have spoiled her by giving in one time too many. The solution is simple—don't let her get her way so often and she will eat the food she is supposed to eat. Of course, an occasional treat never hurt anyone. Whatever the reason is for your cat's finicky behavior, as long as you get to the bottom of what's causing it, you can most likely deal with it and get kitty eating once again.

dislike change of any kind. Humans love to have a variety of food to choose from and would hate to have to eat the same thing for breakfast, lunch, and dinner, but this doesn't seem to bother the typical cat. In fact, a change could horribly upset your feline, and she could go on a hunger strike.

But why would you change your cat's food if she likes what she currently eats? The main reason why cat owners change their cat's food is because a veterinarian recommends it for better health. For example, a cat who has problems with urinary tract blockages may need to switch to a prescription diet. Getting your cat to switch to a new food is not always easy.

It is best to mix her old food with the new food. Gradually increase the amount of new food mixed with the old brand. Over time, your cat will be eating only the new food and will not have noticed the gradual change. Hopefully, kitty will never miss her "old"

Feeding is an important aspect of cat care.

Do not give into your cat's request for "human" food. Your cat can quickly become spoiled.

Cats Not Invited to Dinner

See how cute and pitiful your cat looks when she begs for a small morsel of your dinner? The worst thing you can do is to give in to kitty's pleas and give her a bite of your "human" food. If you give her a chunk of meat today, then why wouldn't you do it again tomorrow? And the next day? And the next? There will be no end in sight. Cats do not think and rationalize like humans do. If they can eat your dinner with you once, then they should be invited to the table every evening. And, they're already dressed for it!

Your cat will let you know when it is time to eat.

food, but if she does notice something is amiss, you may need to slow down the conversion process. Mixing the food, until your cat comes to terms with the fact she has to eat a different diet, will make the conversion to the new food much easier and less stressful for you and your feline.

Loss of Appetite Could be Emotional

Have you ever been really upset over something, such as a death in the family, and refused to eat? Sadness and emotional upset can cause anyone, human or animal, to lose his or her appetite. If something in your household has changed, such as a new person moving in, or even a person or other animal moving out, this can cause such emotional upset for your cat that she might appear finicky for a while. Try to help her through this rough time and offer her something you know she will eat (such as a favorite treat) to get her started again. If your cat doesn't start eating after a few days, you should consult your veterinarian, or an animal behaviorist, and try to correct the changes (if humanly possible) that caused the upset in the first place.

Feeding your cat should not be seen as a "chore." As long as kitty is getting the correct nutrients and happily eats her meals, then you should sit back, enjoy your furry friend, and look forward to sharing many happy years with her. Or, as your cat might say, "Eat, drink, and be 'hairy!'"

Litter Box Training

The litter box…probably one of the greatest inventions in history–if you are a cat owner. As most cat owners know, if kitty uses her litter box, all is right with the world; if she doesn't use it, you are in for many a sleepless night. Luckily, most cats do use their litter boxes, and if they do not use them there is probably a logical explanation. You must think like a cat when you look at where your litter box is placed, how clean and attractive looking it is, and several other small–but extremely important–facts about training kitty to properly use the litter box!

Location, Location, Location

Almost any cat instinctively knows how to use a litter box. It is a cat's natural instinct to bury its

Proper litter box training and maintenance is crucial to your cat's care.

Part 2

Who Invented Kitty Litter?

Whom can we thank for the invention of cat litter and litter boxes? In the 1940s, people were using big containers filled with sand or ashes for litter boxes. This worked but created some very messy tracking problems. Most feline owners just let kitty go outside to eliminate.

A flourishing businessman, H. Edward Lowe, had a great solution to this problem. Mr. Lowe owned a successful building supply company in Michigan. One day, his neighbor asked him for advice on finding an absorbent material that could be used in his cat's "waste" box. Lowe made the ingenious suggestion of using dried ground clay, a product his father manufactured for soaking up industrial oil spills in factories during the war. Lowe's discovery was the answer and letting cats out of the house to go about their business was no longer necessary.

Over 50 years later, the cat litter industry is a million dollar plus business and is still growing strong. In the late 1980's, Thomas Nelson, a biochemist, discovered clumping kitty litter. Nelson found clays that were dried instead of baked. These clays were very absorbent and would form a clump when a cat urinated on them—this has made life much easier for cat owners when it is time for "scooping" the litter box.

The bathroom is a common location for the litter box.

waste in soil or litter. Believe it or not, you won't have to "teach" a feline how to use the litter box. When you introduce your new cat into your house, the first place you should show her is where the litter box is located. Once you've shown the cat where the box is, don't move it around. Pick a spot and leave it, or else kitty might decide to use her favorite "bathroom" location whether the box is there or not.

But where should you put the litter box in the first place? A busy, noisy area might make a shy or modest kitten decide to hide (in such quiet places as under your bed or behind the couch) when she does her very private business. Putting the litter box in an out-of-the-way place to begin with will solve a lot of problems before they have a chance to get started.

Bathrooms are common locations for litter boxes, as are closets, spare bedrooms, basements, or any place that is not in direct contact with your family's daily activities. Find a secluded place for the litter box (or boxes) and everyone will be happy.

Depending on where your feline lives (is it a one room apartment or an entire tri-level house?), you may need more than one litter box. If your cat is at one end of the house when the urge strikes and the litter box is up two flights of stairs at the other end of the house, kitty may have an "accident" before she gets to the box.

If you have more than one cat, the general rule is to have one litter box per cat. Cats don't like sharing their box with each other, although in a multi-cat household, the dominant cat will usually "mark" all the boxes in the home to show who is in charge. Regardless, the more boxes, the better.

Litter Plus Box Equals "Litterbox"

The type of litter you use is just as crucial as the box itself. With very young kittens, it might be better to stay away from the clumping types of litter for a while. There have been instances where tiny kittens could not properly groom themselves and have had the clumps stick to the fur on their behind (which sometimes caused an obstruction and is painful).

Can You Train Kitty to Use a Regular Toilet?

Yes, as impossible as it may seem, you can train your cat to use your toilet as her kitty litter box. Of course, time and patience demands that the transition from litter box to toilet be accomplished in a series of stages. There are kits you can purchase at most pet supply stores that instruct you exactly how—step by step—to transform your cat from ordinary litter box user to sophisticated toilet patron.

If at any time your feline friend gives the whole thing up and urinates elsewhere, you're pushing her too fast and need to slow down the process. Obviously, not every cat is going to be able (or want) to learn this easy-to-clean up-after (with just a flush) feat, so do not force an unwilling, or unable, cat to do this.

It is important to realize that cats are creatures of habit. They don't appreciate change in their nine lives. There are many different brands and types of kitty litter. What you choose is up to you and your cat but, be aware, the first litter you use may condition your kitten to associate only that kind, style, smell, texture, etc., with the kind of litter suitable for eliminating in.

The Different Types of Cat Litter

Paper—Paper litter filling looks and feels like regular clay litters, but is made with recycled paper and is dust-free. Some cat owners make their own litter by purchasing unprinted newspaper at their local printing press, (the ink used to print newspapers could be toxic to kitty), much as cat owners did in the early days before traditional cat litter was invented.

Non-Clumping Clay Litter—Non-clumping cat litter is made from absorbent clay, which is probably the most natural of all litter types. Some brands are dust-free or dust-reduced. There is also a selection of scented and unscented litters. If you use a non-clumping litter, throw away the entire contents of the litter box to ensure a fresh box.

Clumping Litter—Introduced in 1989, clumping litter has become one of the most popular litter types. The smaller granules found in this litter bond or "clump" together when they come in contact with liquid, making waste removal quick, easy, and convenient for the owner.

Cat Litter Pearls—A process transforms natural silica sand into cat litter pearls. The result is a cat litter that absorbs liquid waste in seconds, without clumping, and then allows it to evaporate while odor is locked inside. Litter box pearls are unscented, non-toxic, 100% natural and completely biodegradable. They are designed to save money because you'll use less litter and change the litter you do use less frequently.

Crystal Cat Litter—This revolutionary litter, which is made from silica gel, is super-absorbent and highly effective in controlling cat box odor. Each granule is covered with micro pores that evaporate moisture and trap odor. In fact, a 3.5 pound box of crystal litter lasts up to 30 days for one cat.

Some cats do not like to use enclosed litter boxes. Choose a style your cat prefers.

A change in brands or type of litter has caused even the most well-adjusted cats to stop using their litter boxes and start using other areas in which to eliminate. Buying a certain brand of litter because it is on sale can start the nasty habit of your cat deciding not to use her litter box. If you find a good brand of litter that your cat likes (i.e. uses), your best bet is to stick with that particular litter to avoid any problems later.

Many litter manufacturers make different litter formulas designed to solve specific problems. For example, there are litters that are supposed to act immediately upon the scratching action of kitty and start combating odors from the start. Other types of litter are made specifically for multiple cat households. Litters can be dust-free, chemical-free, fragrance-free, fragrance-filled, clumping, non-clumping, etc. If you can imagine it, there probably is a litter for it!

Choosing a Litter Box

As far as choosing the litter box itself, litter boxes with hoods are probably the best choice because some cats stand inside the litter box but eliminate outside of it. A litter box hood will prevent this as well as give kitty her much-needed privacy. Note, however, that some cats may exhibit signs of claustrophobia and will not enter a litter box that has a hood on it. Therefore, you will have to adjust your plan according to your cat's idea of what is suitable and what is not.

Kittens need a smaller-sized litter box than one designed for adult cats.

Kittens need a different sized litter box than an adult cat. Your kitten's first litter box should be shallow enough that she can easily climb in and out of it. As the kitten grows into an adult, you can adjust the size of the box accordingly.

If Your Cat Stops Using the Litter Box

Nothing is more frustrating for a cat owner than a cat who stops using the litter box, especially if your cat is several years old and has been using the litter box faithfully up until now. What has caused this sudden departure from proper feline bathroom etiquette?

There are several reasons why your cat would suddenly abandon everything she learned in

Do Not Punish Your Cat

It is absolutely reprehensible to rub your feline's nose or face in her accidents (as some people have done in the past) to try to stop this behavior. Cats do not understand punishments such as this, and scolding your cat will only encourage her to hide her accidents to avoid further punishment.

Your cat may refuse to use a smelly litter box. Keep your cat happy by keeping the box clean.

Cleanliness is Crucial

It does not take a feline genius to figure out that a clean litter box is more desirable than one that has not been changed for weeks and smells worse than the two-week-old carton of milk in your refrigerator! Cats have always been known as super-clean, fastidious animals. Purchase an inexpensive scooper that you can use to dispose of solid waste daily, but be sure to change the litter as often as necessary. Cleaning the box on a regular basis is good for everyone in the long run.

"Litter Box Training 101" and choose your soft, fluffy bed pillow as her new portable potty of choice. It may take some detective work from you, however, to figure out what exactly is your cat's peculiar behavior.

Take the Cat to the Veterinarian

The first thing you should do when such a change takes place in your cat's behavior is to take her to the veterinarian as soon as possible. There are numerous medical reasons why your cat would stop using her litter box; the main reason she does so is to make her devoted owners aware that something is definitely wrong. Cats are not dumb. What better way is there to tell you there's a problem than to leave a "kitty calling card" in an obscure location? Now she has your attention!

Why Did Kitty Stop Using Her Litter Box?

An ill feline will most likely try to communicate her pain by inappropriately eliminating (whether defecating or urinating) away from the litter box. In fact, the number one reason cats stop urinating in their litter boxes is because they are sick, usually with a painful lower urinary tract infection. By urinating in strange places, your cat is trying to tell you something.

The Facts About Toxoplasmosis

Toxoplasmosis is a disease caused by an intestinal parasite, Toxoplasma. Cats commonly get the parasite by ingesting raw meat or contaminated prey. Humans can get the disease from handling infected fecal material, so be sure to wear gloves and/or wash your hands after cleaning the litter box. (Pregnant women are advised to avoid changing litter boxes because the disease could harm the unborn child.) Feline symptoms of toxoplasmosis are loss of appetite, fever, and trouble breathing. If you suspect your cat may have toxoplasmosis, take her to the vet as soon as possible.

√ Toxoplasmosis affecting babies is quite rare. The incidence in the US is 0.028% of all births.

√ Keeping your cat indoors so she cannot catch mice will prevent her from contracting toxoplasmosis.

√ Transmission of toxoplasmosis from your cat to you requires that you swallow the toxo organisms that have incubated in your cat's feces for one to five days. Reasonable personal hygiene should be adequate to prevent that from occurring.

√ Testing your cat's blood for toxoplasma antibodies is only meaningful if a positive test is followed two to four weeks later with another test.

√ Weekly testing of your cat's feces will detect if your cat is capable of transmitting toxoplasmosis.

√ Toxoplasmosis is transmitted more often in the US by poorly cooked meat than by exposure to kitty litter boxes and the waste found in them.

A cat cannot tell you if it hurts to urinate. Unfortunately, the only way she can get your attention is by changing her litter box habits and hoping you figure out that something is indeed very wrong. Remember, do not punish her for her actions. As with cats that defecate outside the litter box, if your veterinarian gives kitty a clean bill of health, you will have to look elsewhere for the cause, which is most likely behavioral.

Of course, any of the reasons listed for cats inappropriately urinating away from their litter boxes is also true for inappropriate defecation problems. A new addition to the family might upset your cat enough to change her behavior. Whether the addition is another person or a fellow feline, kitty's confusion at this change may lead her to start eliminating in other places. This is especially true if another feline begins using the cat's litter box, which is a very territorial place. The general rule is to have one litter box per cat. With luck, the adjustment period will be short for your non-litter box user.

Part 2

If there have been any changes in your household, including new additions (either animal or human), if you've recently moved, changed brands of litter, haven't cleaned the box, or perhaps you've had a slight change in your schedule or routine, it can cause your feline to develop stress-related litter box issues.

Techniques to Get Kitty Back to the Box

If your cat has seen the veterinarian and received a clean bill of health, then something else (either psychological or environmental) is causing her to shun the litter box. Any changes in litter brands or even the location of the litter box might upset your cat and cause her not to want to use the box anymore. In cases such as this, the main objective is to retrain your feline to use the box again.

One proven technique is to put your cat's food bowl in the location where she has been having her accidents (cats usually will not defecate where they eat) and, if you have to, place her in a small room with nothing but food, water, and her litter box so she will learn to use the box again. Never place a litter box in a heavily-traveled or busy part of the house. This only causes a shy or skittish cat to look for a more private potty spot.

Remember that cats are fastidiously clean animals. A dirty, smelly litter box will make kitty look for cleaner quarters. Anything and everything that you can do to encourage your cat to use her litter box should be a priority to keep everyone in your home as happy and as comfortable as possible.

If your cat should have an "accident" do not punish her. Try to find out what is wrong.

Neutralizing Kitty Odors

The odor of cat urine is much like that of harsh ammonia. Fortunately, kitty litter has been designed to soak up and absorb the pungent fragrance of cat urine. What if, however, your cat isn't using the place in which you put your absorbing cat litter? What if kitty is urinating somewhere (or everywhere) other than the litter box?

Cat urine odor removers fall into three basic categories: enzymatic, bacterial, and chemical. Each of these is more or less effective, depending on factors such as the "freshness" of the stains and odors. Cat urine odors and stains have a way of lingering forever if not treated quickly. However, please remember that the worst possible mistake is to use an ammonia-based cleaner, as cats will only return to the scent because feline urine has a very similar smell.

The most important thing to remember about cat urine is "get it while it's fresh." Urine goes through a decaying process as it "ages" in your carpet. Bacteria feed on the organic wastes, converting them into gases, primarily that strong ammonia smell. Aside from the developing odor, the longer you allow urine to remain, the greater its chances are of seeping through the carpet and into the pad and/or the wood floor beneath.

Fresh urine can often be cleaned up by following these steps:

• Blot–Use an old, thick, bath towel and blot up as much liquid as you can. Continue to blot with paper towels until no moisture is seen.

• Dilute and Blot Again–Heavily spray the area with water or a mild solution of white vinegar and water, then blot again.

• Neutralize–If the odor still exists after the carpet is completely dry, it's time to break out the big guns: use odor removers based on chemicals,

Which Litter is Best?

If you're unsure which type of litter your cat would prefer, why not set up several boxes, side by side, with different litter types in each? This test will allow the cat to make her preference clear so you can oblige her in the future. Litter box training can be simple and stress-free for both you and your cat if you follow kitty's lead. If you have trained your cat correctly and followed all of the litter box "rules and regulations," there should be a happy cat in your household.

Using Black Lights to Find Urine Accidents

Nothing is more frustrating than searching for the cause of cat urine odor. Black light technology makes use of special ultra-violet rays that are on the same wavelength as biological waste, such as cat urine, turning a tedious task into a breeze. Several companies have manufactured urine locaters to help search out the source of that very distinct odor. Your local pet store should carry these lights.

Part 2

Part 2

As a general rule, each cat in the household should have his or her own litter box.

To Cover or Not To Cover

Do you have one cat in your multi-cat household that does not cover up her waste after using the litter box? Since cats are territorial, there is always a dominant feline in the group and, often, this cat will not cover up her waste so the other cats will be aware of her presence. The reason cats bury their waste is to cover their scent from predators. Interestingly enough, if you have a one-cat household and kitty still doesn't bury her waste, this means your fearless feline thinks you need to be reminded of who is dominant in the household.

enzymes, or bacteria/enzymes, designed to neutralize the odor by eating, up the bacteria causing it.

For old and dried urine stains in carpeting, the bacterial process is well underway and you will most likely need the help of some top-notch odor removal products. Ask advice from fellow cat owners as well as the sales staff at your local pet store. It is important to follow the manufacturer's directions on the package for best results in removing these stains and odors.

Be aware that if the urine soaked all the way through to the underlying wood floor you may need to remove the carpet and padding, and treat the wood directly. Then you'll have to make the decision to attempt to save your existing carpet (you may need the assistance of a professional cleaner) or re-carpet entirely.

Litter box training is important for cats and their owners. Remember to keep the box clean at all times and place it in a quiet location of your home. Your cat will thank you by using the box every time!

Grooming for Cats and Kittens

Cat hair. Sometimes you think you've seen enough of it to last you a lifetime. And as you're picking it off your black slacks or new coat, hair by single hair, you wish you *had* seen the last of it. However, the seemingly "magnetic" substance that appears to be an integral part of every cat lover's home is actually a crucial element of your feline's entire makeup. This essential ingredient is your cat's fur coat (or hair). If you've ever lived with a cat, you know that cat hair does not stay on kitty forever, but falls off–a process known as shedding.

The Hairy Truth

To anyone who has ever examined a cat, it's evident that all cats do not look the same. Many factors are involved in the overall appearance of a feline, but

A well-groomed cat makes an attractive, happy pet.

Part 2

The Long (And Short) of Cat Hair

Even though short-haired breeds require much less grooming, the largest number of cats registered in the US happen to be long-haired! According to the Cat Fanciers' Association (CFA), the world's largest purebred registry, only 10 out of the 40 eligible breeds of felines are classified as long-haired cats. Although it would seem that the short-haired feline is more popular, nothing could be further from the truth.

Long-haired cats may have hairs up to five inches long, while in contrast, a short-haired feline may have hairs measuring less than two inches. CFA statistics counted over 30,000 very hairy Persians registered in their association, accounting for nearly two-thirds of the total number of CFA registered cats.

CFA's number two spot also goes to a long-hair—the mammoth-sized Maine Coon. What's surprising about the Maine Coon's numbers is that the statistics show only 4,500 registered—a startling difference of almost 25,000 felines between the number one and two popularity positions. About two-thirds of the total registered purebreds in the CFA are graced with a surplus of hair. Apparently, the long-haired varieties of our little furry friends are the decided favorites among feline fanciers.

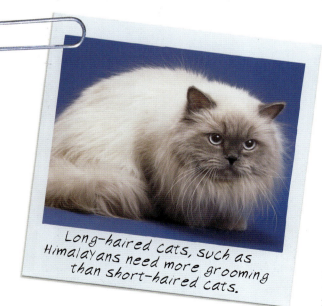

Long-haired cats, such as Himalayans need more grooming than short-haired cats.

the coat is the most obvious. Color and pattern, of course, play an important role, but the length, type, number, and texture of each precious hair on kitty's body recounts an intriguing story about the evolution of the cat.

Cats have been blessed with an assortment of hair follicles designed to, among other things, protect and assist them in their environment. Your cat's fur coat helps insulate her against the elements.

When the Fur Flies

Just as humans grow and lose hair, felines exhibit similar hair growth and loss cycles. Shedding is part of the normal hair growth cycle in cats. Each hair follicle goes through a sequence of active growth (anagen), transition (catagen), and rest (telogen). As new hairs grow in, the old ones are pushed out, thus causing the unpopular, yet very necessary, act of shedding.

Most cat owners living in seasonal climates have probably noticed that their cats seem to grow a "winter coat," when the colder months begin. Then, as the warmer days of spring approach, kitty gradually sheds her coat just as humans trade in their bulky winter wardrobes for their lighter summer ones. The change in the temperatures, however, is not the factor that promotes the growth and shedding cycles.

Shedding is directly caused by photoperiod changes, or the amount of daylight in the area. Thus, indoor cats that live where you keep the lights on even though it is dark outside, will shed differently than outdoor cats in seasonal climates. Usually, cats stop shedding in winter because there is less light—not because of the change in temperatures (although retaining her fur helps kitty keep warm). Indoor cats never really stop shedding; they just do it all the time in lesser amounts.

Taking Control

The most important thing you can do to cut back on the airborne, stick-to-everything cat hair is to institute a regular grooming schedule. Whether you comb and brush your feline at home or let a professional groomer wrestle it out with kitty, grooming needs to be done. Your cat will be much happier if she has help in removing excess hair that can cause serious problems, including hairballs that can lead to vomiting and/or constipation.

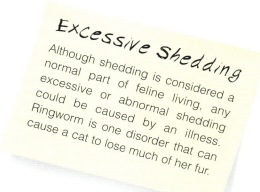

Excessive Shedding

Although shedding is considered a normal part of feline living, any excessive or abnormal shedding could be caused by an illness. Ringworm is one disorder that can cause a cat to lose much of her fur.

Part 2

The "hairless" Sphynx cat requires less grooming than other breeds.

Part 2

It's easy to groom your cat at home. Your cat will learn to enjoy the extra attention.

Hairballs

With varied hair lengths comes a health problem you'll need to be aware of—hairballs. Long-haired cats seem to suffer more from hairballs and the ailments associated with them. The hair your cat ingests while grooming herself usually passes through her system without harm. Sometimes cats will vomit up the hair they've swallowed. This is normal. If you think your cat may have hairballs, feeding her "cat grass" will help her regurgitate any excess hair. Laxatives, such as mineral oil or vegetable oil may help as well. You can also apply a small amount of mayonnaise or butter to the cat's paws. As she ingests it, the oil will loosen the hairballs. Hairballs can cause constipation. In severe cases, the intestines or stomach may become blocked with hair and veterinary care is required to remedy the problem. The more fur your cat has, the more hair she will ingest during grooming.

Whether your cat sheds all the time or some of the time, loses tons of fur or just an occasional hair every now and then, understanding the importance of the shedding process might make dealing with the hair somewhat less troublesome. And when your cat curls up on your lap at night and bestows upon you the greatest of honors–letting you stroke those luxurious layers upon layers of feline fur–you'll realize that dealing with a little cat hair is more than worth the trade-off.

Grooming Your Cat at Home

You may be asking yourself, "If cats are such great groomers, why would they need any help?" There are several answers to that question. An unkempt cat should be an immediate signal to any cat owner that a visit to the veterinarian is necessary. Sometimes, the only symptoms of illness shown by your cat may be the way she looks–dirty, sloppy, and generally ungroomed.

For grooming a kitten or cat, you will need:

√ a brush and comb (the types differ for long-haired and short-haired cats)

√ special nail clippers for cats (which you can get at a pet store or from your veterinarian)

√ a little kitty toothbrush and toothpaste (which can be found at a pet store or obtained from your veterinarian's office).

√ cotton balls

√ stypic pencil

You can find all the grooming tools you need at your local pet supply store.

It would be easy to assume, that since cats lived on their own for centuries before they became domesticated, that they would not need human assistance with grooming. Unfortunately, this is not true. A lot of cats are not capable of properly grooming themselves. If they are sick, old, or in a climate they are not bred for (such as the Norwegian Forest Cat living in Miami, Florida), kitty will need help with grooming.

Another reason a feline may appear to be ungroomed is that she is getting older and cannot keep up her tidy appearance as she did in her younger years. Grooming an older cat (or any feline, for that matter) has an added benefit–routine grooming and hands-on attention will assist in the early detection of external parasites (such as fleas and ticks), tumors, infections, or any other changes or abnormalities that may result from an internal disease condition. Simply put, by having your cat groomed, you could save her life.

Cats of all shapes and sizes may need assistance with grooming–no matter how much fur they have. For instance, Persians and Himalayans, Maine Coons, and other long-haired cats could have some difficulties keeping up with all that hair. Coats and undercoats, manes, and ear tufts could prove to be overwhelming for these luxurious-looking creatures.

By their very nature, cats are clean animals. They groom themselves daily.

Some cat owners trim their cat's nails. Your vet can show you how to do it.

The same can be true in short-haired breeds as well—even if they don't have as much hair to contend with.

The key to helping a cat accept your assistance with the grooming process is to start grooming her at a very young age. The most important part of grooming is to make it a good experience for your cat. Perhaps the best thing you can do for a kitten is to take out that comb and get her used to it, even before she really needs it.

A secret to grooming is to convince your feline that grooming time is also a "bonding" time with her favorite human, so try to make it a fun and rewarding time for both of you. Both you and your cat want the same thing—for her to be clean. That goal can be reached with a lot of patience and a little time invested in your kitty.

Trimming the Nails

Before the grooming process begins you may want to trim your cat's nails to prevent getting scratched. You should trim a cat's claws approximately once a month. Place the cat in your lap and while securely holding her, gently press down on the paw so the nail comes out. With a pair of clippers, clip off the tip of each claw just outside the pinkish part where the nerves are.

Always have a styptic pencil on hand when clipping your cat's nails. If you accidentally cut into the quick, the nail will bleed. Applying the styptic pencil, or light, direct pressure, will stop the bleeding. Give your cat time to calm down if you've cut into the quick, as she will most likely be

Declawing

The declawing issue has been a major source of controversy among cat lovers for some time. One of most cat owners' biggest "bad kitty" complaints is scratching. You love all the furnishings and collectibles in your home. When you start finding your valuables scratched up and/or shredded, you begin contemplating a solution. Cats need to scratch to keep their nails healthy, and, although declawing is a permanent solution to a scratching problem, it is an inhumane procedure.

Some veterinarians will refuse to do the surgery necessary to declaw a cat. Besides making the creature utterly defenseless, it can also cause serious psychological problems (i.e., many declawed cats fight back by biting, become depressed, or overly aggressive). Clipping your cat's nails often and teaching kitty to use the scratching post are much more humane methods of deterring your cat from bad scratching habits.

Part 2

too upset for you to finish the grooming procedure. If you feel uncomfortable about performing this procedure, your veterinarian or local groomer can do this for a small fee. Once the nails have been clipped, you are ready to groom your cat.

Grooming Time

Although most cats will need an occasional brushing or combing, long-haired felines are more in need of help with this task. Their hair tangles easily and can get soiled or get debris knotted in it. If the cat goes outside, burrs and stickers can get caught in the cat's fur and may be almost impossible for your cat to get out by herself. The best way to avoid matted fur and heavy shedding is to stop these problems before they start. Regular grooming will become your salvation.

Start grooming your cat at a young age. The cat will enjoy spending time with you.

As stated earlier, starting the daily grooming regimen when the cat is young will make it easier for both of you in the years that follow. It will be

Removing Tar, Paint, or Oil From Feline Fur

A cat can get into many unpleasant substances that will need to be removed frcm her coat. It is important to stress that cat owners should never use gasoline, turpentine, kerosene, paint remover, or similar substances to remove tar, paint, or oil from a cat's coat. Small amounts of tar or paint can carefully be cut out of the coat. Large amounts of tar can be removed by soaking the affected fur in vegetable oil or mineral oil for 24 hours, then using soap and water to wash off the substance.

Cornstarch can be sprinkled on smaller patches of oil and then brushed off. As a last resort in cases where the entire animal is covered in oil, shampoo your cat with a gentle dishwashing detergent, and follow up with a cat shampoo. If your cat has gotten into something really sticky or oily, you may need to have her professionally groomed.

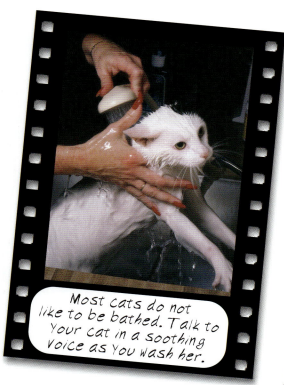

Most cats do not like to be bathed. Talk to your cat in a soothing voice as you wash her.

helpful to have two types of combs—one fine-toothed and one with wide teeth. Comb your cat to remove any tangles. (Long-haired cats may need to have tangles removed by hand so the brush or comb does not pull them out. Only cut a knot out as a last resort, and be careful not to let the scissors touch the cat's skin, which pierces easily.) You can use a bristle brush or a soft acrylic brush to smooth out your cat's coat. (Always brush the fur in the natural direction in which it lies.) Removing the excess fur from your feline's coat will not only prevent her from getting hairballs, but brushing stimulates circulation and helps keep your cat's coat shiny and healthy looking.

Bathing Your Cat

Most cats hate water and there is not a lot you can do to change that fact. There are some felines who do not mind a little H_2O now and then. For example, the Turkish Van is known as a great admirer of the wet stuff and even loves to swim. All in all, cats and water do not mix well, but if you start bathing your kitten early in life and get her used to the experience, it can make all the difference between dealing with a calm and relaxed cat or a ferocious cyclone of claws, teeth, and wet fur.

Put a mat on the bottom of the sink to help prevent the cat from slipping. (This will make her feel more secure in her footing.) When bathing a cat, always keep your hands in the water flow so you can detect any change in the water temperature. An affectionate cat could innocently rub up against the faucet controls and change the water temperature, leading to serious burns.

You can also wear thick gloves if you anticipate kitty may get a little rambunctious during the bath and try to scratch or bite you. Some cat owners even put a piece of screen in the sink or bathtub so that kitty has something to hang onto (or claw profusely) instead of your arms or hands.

You may need the help of a friend to hold the cat firmly but gently in the sink or tub. (Your cat may not like being bathed and could squirm and put up a fuss. Talk calmly to her and reassure her that everything's fine.) Fill the sink with a few inches of lukewarm water and lightly wet the cat. Rub in a small amount of shampoo and begin working it through the cat's coat. Use a mild shampoo designed for cats (your vet can recommend one for you) and avoid getting any water or soap into kitty's ears or eyes. Rinse the cat with warm water until all traces of soap are gone from her coat.

Only bathe your cat when absolutely necessary, such as if she's been sprayed by a skunk or has gotten something oily or foul in her fur. (If you show your cat, however, you will have to bathe her before each cat show to ensure she looks perfect for the show ring.)

Skunky Encounters of the Smelly Kind

In the unlikely event that your cat gets into a "spraying war" with a skunk, you won't have any trouble figuring out what happened once you get a whiff of that unmistakable skunk scent. You also won't have much trouble figuring out who lost the war.

There are many commercial products on the market to remove skunk stains and smells. However, you can start by shampooing your cat and then pour either milk or tomato juice directly on her fur and let it soak for approximately ten minutes before rinsing well.

If your cat scratches her ears a lot she may have ear mites.

Dry the cat off with a soft, fluffy towel and keep her away from drafts until she has dried completely. Do not let your cat go outside when wet, as she may catch a chill. Some cats may tolerate being dried with a hairdryer. If you do this, be sure to use a low setting and keep the hairdryer several inches away from the cat to prevent burns.

In addition to grooming the cat's coat, you should also take a few extra minutes to groom your cat's eyes, ears, and teeth.

Ears

Be sure to clean your cat's ears whenever you groom her. The ears should be clean and free from any dark, waxy residue. Swab out the ear area with a clean cotton ball dampened with a bit of baby oil. Cats have very sensitive and delicate ears, so handle them carefully. Do not stick anything into the cat's ear canal, as you can damage the eardrum. Consult your veterinarian if you think your cat has ear mites or if the ears smell foul. The vet can provide medication to eliminate these problems.

Eyes

A cat's eyes require very little attention during grooming. If your cat has runny eyes, gently wipe any discharge away with a cotton ball dampened with warm water.

Teeth

Good dental hygiene is important to your cat's overall health and well-being. Brushing your cat's teeth is an important part of the grooming process. Plaque and tartar build up on the cat's teeth over time and should be removed. Start brushing your

You can swab the area around your cat's eyes with a soft cotton ball.

cat's teeth at an early age to accustom her to the procedure. Gently open kitty's mouth and examine the teeth. The gums should appear pink and healthy. Any signs of swollen or bleeding gums, or broken or loose teeth, should be brought to the attention of your veterinarian immediately. Only use toothpaste designed for cats (your vet can recommend one for you). Human toothpaste may make your cat ill. Rub the teeth gently with a cat toothbrush, and be sure to get the gums too.

Wanted: Professional Cat Groomer

Choosing a groomer for your cat is much like choosing a hairdresser for yourself. Most people don't just close their eyes and randomly pick a phone number in the yellow pages. You usually start asking around and finding out who your friends and relatives take their business to. The same should be the case when finding a kitty stylist. Your veterinarian should be

Dental care is important. Examine your cat's teeth before you brush them.

Groomers Who Make House Calls

In our highly active lifestyles, it is no surprise that there are numerous mobile pet groomers. A fully equipped van will pull up to your front door, and the groomer will give your cat a professional grooming in no time. Ask your local veterinarian or check you phone book for a groomer who makes house calls in your area.

Brushing improves circulation and makes your cat's coat smooth and shiny.

Part 2

An older cat or one who goes outside often may need extra help in grooming.

Finding a Groomer in Your Area

You can find a qualified groomer in your area by consulting the *Find A Groomer Annual World Directory 2002*
The Madson Group, Inc.,
Dept. PetGroomer.com
13775 A Mono Way, Suite 224
Sonora, CA 95370
Phone: (209) 532-5222
Fax: (209) 532-7272
Website:
http://www.findagroomer.com

able to recommend a good groomer whose work they have witnessed on their patients. Your vet might even have an in-house professional groomer service for you to visit. Check the references of any groomer you decide to use.

It's important to groom your cat at least once a week. Long-haired cats may need to be brushed or combed every day. Grooming is one way to check your cat for any parasites, wounds, or other signs of illness. It also is a good time to bond with your cat and give her extra attention and love. Although your cat may not take to being groomed right away, she will soon see the benefits of having her human companion fuss over her, and may even insist on being brushed just to get extra attention. With regular grooming, your cat will not only look better; she'll feel better too. Take the time to keep your cat looking her best at all times and she will reward you with a contented purr at the end of the day.

Part Three
Your Cat at Home

"You may want to keep your cat indoors, Ma'am. I caught ol' Baxter here
with plans to vandalize city hall."

Multiple Cat Households

According to statistics compiled from the American Pet Products Manufacturers Association's (APPMA) 2001-2002 National Pet Owners Survey, three out of ten (or about 35 million) households own at least one feline. Out of those 35 million homes, almost half house two or more cats. The study concluded that the average cat-populated dwelling has approximately two cats sharing the home. (Of course, that means the other half of cat owners have only one cat companion living with them.) The statistics of cat adoptions, as well as the popularity of felines, have steadily increased over the past few decades mainly because of the cat's "independent" lifestyle which is welcome in today's busy world.

The average household in the US has two cats.

Two cats will play together and keep each other company.

If you are one of the people in that fifty percent of single cat homes, have you ever consider adopting a buddy or two for kitty? Although cats are not considered pack animals, unlike their canine counterparts, they still can get lonely, especially if you are gone much of the day. Although your cat would like you to think she is totally self-sufficient, the truth is that getting a second (or third, or fourth) cat would probably enrich your cat's life many times over.

Cat Introductions

Introducing one cat to another cat isn't quite as simple as dog-to-dog introductions. Cats are extremely territorial, as well as very envious, when the limelight shines on anything other than them. When bringing a cat into a home with an existing kitty, you need to consistently reassure the first cat that she isn't being replaced but, instead, having the chance to make a new furry friend.

Part 3

A proper introduction, obviously, is the crucial point when bringing a new cat into your home. When introducing cats to each other, owners should always be present in case any fighting occurs–especially when one pet is a tiny kitten and the other is an adult. When you can't be there, one good way to get cats used to one another is to keep them in separate, but adjoining rooms so they can at least smell each other and touch paws underneath a closed door. No one gets hurt this way, and the felines will learn (hopefully) to accept each other.

You can also use a travel crate to introduce the cats to one another. Put the newcomer in a travel crate and set it on the floor. The established cat will more than likely come over to investigate the new addition to the household. After a short time, switch the cats; put the established cat in the crate and allow the new cat to wander around the room and meet and greet her new housemate. This method will allow the cats to see and sniff each other, but will prevent any fighting.

With time, patience, and tons of extra attention given to everyone (especially the resident cat or cats) having enough love to go around for each and every cat is essential. Getting them used to each other really isn't that difficult and staying together as a family for many years is what makes the pet family so fortunate.

Believe it or not, the world of cats is very much like a royal or political hierarchy. There is always a cat "in charge" and she rules the roost, so to speak. Usually, the dominant cat is a male, although a colony of altered cats may have a female holding

Allow the new cat to meet and greet the established cat.

There is always one cat "in charge" or ruling the roost.

Part 3

In time, the cats will learn to get along and start to play with each other.

Cat Collecting

Cat "collectors" are not to be confused with legitimate cat rescue groups. The former (no matter how well-meaning they are) seem to suffer from some type of eccentricity that causes them to take in more cats than they can handle, which often results in masses of ill-fed, unaltered, and some very sick cats living in horrid conditions.

True cat rescuers, on the other hand, have the resources to properly feed and care for the cats they rescue. Normally, they provide a stopping-off place where the animal can be restored to health, receive veterinary care, and be spayed or neutered before being adopted out to a permanent home.

Authorities cannot do a house-to-house search to ensure that animals are properly cared for; they depend heavily on reports by the public. If you see a situation involving animals that just doesn't look "right" chances are it isn't. You don't need to be an investigator—leave that to the proper authorities.

the top spot. When cats are introduced, one will usually know immediately whether or not she is the dominant cat. The submissive cat, when meeting the "top cat," will stand her ground for a minute or two worth of howls and growls, but will eventually slink off to sulk.

The sense of smell is very important in the animal world. Cats use scent markers to claim their territory. When introducing two cats that you want to get along and live together peacefully, it is not uncommon to use that sense of smell as a bargaining tool. Some people will put a drop of a fragranced non-toxic soap or shampoo or vanilla extract on the back of kitty's neck or tail. Putting the same smell on both cats makes them think that if they smell alike, they must be alike.

Replaced?

A cat that is particularly attached to her owner might feel slighted when a new cat arrives in the house, especially if she has been the "only cat" and has never shared the home with another cat. She might feel jealous or unloved, particularly if the new cat is a bouncy, adorable kitten. Reassure your cat that she is not being replaced by giving her lots of extra attention and love. Play with her as much as you can and let her know that she not being "replaced" by the other cat, but merely sharing her home with a new friend.

Give the original cat extra love and attention so she won't feel neglected or left out.

One of the best ways to get two cats to like (or at least tolerate) each other is to play with them together. Get out some kitty toys and start throwing, wiggling, rolling them, or whatever it takes to make the cat forget she's ticked off about a strange cat invading her space. Pretty soon, the two cats will be playing with the toys and then, before they even know what happened, playing with each other.

If you have multiple cats in your household it's a good idea to give each cat his or her own litter box, food dishes, and toys. Even if the cats get along fine with each other, they may not want to "share" their toys or stand in line at the food dish. Older, or more aggressive cats have been known to intimidate the newcomer away from the food dish at mealtimes; one food dish per cat will solve this problem.

Fighting

If you introduce a new cat into your household, established cats may feel threatened by the newcomer (even if she is an innocent kitten) and you should prepare yourself for some minor squabbling. All cats react to change differently; some will welcome a new friend or playmate while others may become jealous. The cats may hiss and growl upon first introduction, but after a few days they should become accustomed to each other. If any serious fighting occurs, however, separate the cats and give them time to cool off. Try reintroducing them, under supervised conditions, until they start to get along. Never leave two cats that are aggressive toward each other alone unsupervised.

Part 3

Each cat in the household should have his or her own feeding dish and litter box to prevent squabbling.

Every Cat Knows its Nose is Unique

Every cat's nose pad, (also called nose leather), has unique characteristics. Just as no two humans have the same fingerprints, it's a fact that no two felines have "noseprints" that are identical.

Having more than one cat in your home doubles the fun and joy of cat ownership.

Some cats are picky about using the litter box and will not use a box that another cat has used because it has the scent of the other cat on it. Cats can be territorial and the established head of the cat household (or alpha cat) will mark the litter box to let the other cats in the house know who's in charge. A litter box for each cat will keep everyone happy and prevent any litter box "accidents."

Multiple cat households can (and do) exist under the most ideal of circumstances. If you currently only own one cat, please consider adopting a new friend for your best friend. Living with more than one cat companion can bring much joy as well as double the enormous amount of love that already exists in your heart. Hopefully, there is room for just one more.

Keeping Your Cat Safe

Although many people believe cats can take care of themselves, there are dangers present both in and out of the home. As a responsible cat owner, you should do all you can to ensure the health and safety of your cat.

One of the easiest ways to keep your cat safe is to keep her indoors. This of course sparks the indoors versus outdoors debate among cat owners. This topic can cause a heated discussion among the calmest of cat lovers. Is there a correct answer to this question? Can both camps be completely satisfied? Probably not, but each side has strong opinions and cat owners most likely will never agree on which is better–your cat living within the safety of your four walls or roaming "free" in the great outdoors.

Cats can find new ways to get into trouble. Do all you can to keep your cat safe.

Part 3

Keeping your cat indoors will lower the risk of her becoming injured.

The great outdoors poses many dangers to your cat. Don't let her wander off.

The Great Indoors

The usual position of today's animal shelters is on the side of the indoor cat. It is very clear to see where they are coming from because they are trying to control the overpopulation of animals. If unaltered pets are free to roam, they can contribute to the already out-of-hand cat overpopulation problem. Keeping your cat inside is safer for the animal, period. It is also a fact that cats that are allowed outside have much shorter lifespans because of all the hazards that exist.

Although keeping your cat indoors will greatly reduce the risk of her being injured, you must take some indoor precautions to ensure your home does not contain any hazards to your pet. Many household plants are poisonous to cats. Find out which ones (if any) you have in your home and make sure your cat does not have access to them. Other household hazards include open flames from fireplaces and candles, rubber bands and other small objects that could be a choking hazard, and even the ribbons and bows used to decorate holiday packages. As long as you cat and kitten proof your home, your feline will be safe and content to spend her days indoors with the people she loves best.

The Not-So-Great Outdoors

There are millions of cat owners—good, caring, and loving people—who believe that the cat, no matter how domesticated it has become, deserves the right of freedom—to run, to play, and to sleep outside in the green grass underneath a big blue sky. Many of these outdoor felines were probably strays that appeared on the owner's doorstep and, since the cats were

> ### Keep In Mind
>
> Plastic grocery bags pose a danger to indoor cats. If your cat plays with or in the bag, the plastic handle could get wrapped around your cat's neck and choke her. Be sure to keep all plastic bags away from your pets.

Monitor your cat closely while she's outside so she doesn't get into any trouble.

already living outside even though they could have come from an indoor home environment, the owners of kitty's newfound "home" decided to feed the cat but not bring it inside. Obviously, this is better than not feeding the cat. However, these cats should be vaccinated and spayed or neutered to help curb the overpopulation problem that currently exists.

Outside, there lies real danger to the well-being and survival of a small, helpless feline. Being hit by a car is one of the major causes of death for a cat who goes outdoors. Other dangers, such as disease, predatory animals (coyotes, dogs, raccoons, or other wild animals), weather hazards, getting hung up in a tree by her collar, hunting traps, and freak accidents (as well as not-so-accidental injuries caused by uncaring people) can prove hazardous to your feline's health and, quite possibly, her life.

Summertime Blues for Indoor and Outdoor Cats

While most of us look forward to the warming temperatures and the long, sunny days of summer, keep in mind that your faithful feline companions depend on you to keep them happy and healthy during the sultry summer months. Whether your cat lives indoors or outdoors, you must be aware of the numerous threats the summer months could present

Part 3

Long-haired cats often become overheated in the summer. Be sure to keep your cat cool.

Summer Grooming

Regular grooming to prevent hair-balls is important at this time of year. During the warmer months cats are shedding their "winter" coats. Getting the excess hair off your cat will help keep her cooler during those extremely hot summer days.

for your cat. But you can protect your unsuspecting feline against such hazards as heatstroke, drowning, poisoning, insect stings and snake bites, sunburn, and other dangers that this season might introduce.

The Cool Cat

A cat's body is quite different from the human body when exposed to extreme heat conditions. While we cool ourselves by perspiring through our sweat glands, cats cannot do this because they have no sweat glands. They cool themselves by licking their fur (which temporarily cools them) and by panting. Cats pant to lose body heat so they can regulate their body temperature. Older cats, overweight cats, and short-nosed cats, such as Persians and Himalayans, suffer the most in extreme heat. Your cat should be closely monitored during dangerously hot weather conditions. Remember, however, that a normal, healthy cat will have the sense to avoid circumstances (such as becoming overactive in excessive temperatures) that could endanger her health.

Your cat's eating patterns will most likely change during the summer months because almost all animals in a heated environment eat less. You should somewhat decrease her food consumption in extreme heat, but there is no need to alter the specific type of food

Your cat will enjoy surveying the outside world from a shady perch.

Quick-Heating Automobiles Dangerous for Pets

NEVER leave your pet in an enclosed, unventilated area, such as a parked vehicle. It has been estimated that with an outside temperature of 85 degrees Fahrenheit, and the car windows open less than two inches, an automobile will heat up to 102 degrees in only ten minutes. After twenty minutes, the temperature can reach 120 degrees. This would prove fatal to a cat or any other pet.

your cat eats. Fresh, cool water (not ice cold) should be available to your cat at all times. Keep an eye on how much water your cat is drinking so you will be aware if she isn't drinking enough, which could lead to dehydration.

Sunbathing Cats

Providing cool and shady spots for your cat during the hot months is essential, no matter where your cat spends her summer days. If your cat lives indoors, remember to leave your air conditioning on for her while you're away. A closed-up house can get very hot when the summer sun is beating down on it. If you don't have air conditioning, at least provide adequate ventilation with fans to allow air passage throughout the house. Remember to keep your cat out of direct sunlight. Keeping the curtains closed can reduce temperatures in the house as well as prevent sunburn.

The main benefit of keeping your cat indoors is that you have much more control over her surroundings. But, in the event that your cat does venture outdoors, make sure that a shaded, cool place is provided for kitty. Whether it is an outside shelter or a cluster of bushes, the cat must have a place to get out of the sun and cool off. Of course, a bowl of fresh water must also be accessible to the cat.

Part 3

Make sure your cat doesn't ingest any lawn care chemicals while outdoors.

Exposure to Lawn Chemicals

Cats are allowed outside more often in the summer when many people are focusing on lawn and garden care. A significant threat to your outdoor cat is the possible exposure to the lawn and garden chemicals you may use. If you use chemicals on your lawn and garden be sure to let your lawn dry completely before allowing your cat (or any pet) to walk on it. One option is to treat your lawn right before it rains so that the chemicals will be rinsed off the surface of your lawn while, at the same time, be embedded into the ground's surface. Another solution for treating your lawn, however, is to use organic remedies.

Summer Fun Could be Dangerous to Kitty

Popular summertime fun may be potentially dangerous for your pet. Many favorite human activities involve water. Whether you are fishing down by the pond, swimming a few laps in the pool, or washing your car with a sudsy bucket of lukewarm water, your innocent cat may fall victim to one of her worst fears–water. If you've ever attempted to bathe a cat, you know cats don't like water. Even though most cats are excellent swimmers, they can very easily drown if they fall into water over their heads and can't find an escape.

Try to keep your cat away from unsupervised situations where deep water is involved. If you have a pool, a fishing pond, a large steel watering tank for livestock, or any other place where your cat may get stuck, make sure there is an accessible exit ramp your cat can use to climb out of the water if she accidentally falls in.

Keeping Kitty Away from the Wild Side

The summer season brings out more wild animals in search of food. Animals such as raccoons, possums, skunks, and even other cats will fight with your domesticated cat. If your cat isn't immunized (and every cat should have the necessary shots), rabies and other deadly diseases could be transmitted to your feline friend.

Part 3

The Cat Breed That Loves Water

Probably a descendent of the once popular Turkish Angora, the Turkish Van has the unusual distinction as the cat that actually likes water. Normally, cats and water do not mix and trying to get your cat into a tub full of water will usually turn unpleasant for both kitty and you. The Turkish Van, however, will be more than delighted to go skinny-dipping in the pool and show you how to swim a few laps like an Olympian feline!

Some barn cats live their entire lives as outdoor cats.

Insects are another nuisance we must deal with during the summer months. Be sure to watch your cat closely when she goes outside and if you see her chasing bees or bugs, don't allow her to play with them. Many types of ants, such as the red fire ant are dangerous. If you spot an anthill, destroy it so your cat doesn't accidentally find herself in the middle of thousands of angry ants.

Preparing for Parasite Invasions

One of the leading dangers to your outside cat is the possible infestation of pests. Ticks, mites, fleas, lice, and other small pests can easily attach themselves to your cat. It is your job to carefully search for any such pests and to rid your pet of them immediately. There are many highly effective flea and tick treatments available on today's market and your veterinarian can recommend a flea and tick control product for you.

Ticks can cause considerable harm if left on your pet and should be removed immediately by taking a pair of tweezers and gently pulling the tick's head (which is buried under your cat's skin) out of the cat. You may also check with your local pet store for special tick-removing tweezers for an easier, more effective way to deal with ticks.

Part 3

If your cat goes outside, she could pick up unwanted pests such as fleas and ticks.

Since the outbreak of Lyme Disease, pet owners have been very nervous about ticks spreading this condition. Fortunately for cat owners, this hasn't been a major problem because cats rarely become infected with Lyme Disease. Although the reason for this is unknown, experts suspect that felines either have a natural immunity or else they groom themselves so well that they remove the ticks before any damage can be done. Still, if you suspect your cat may have contracted Lyme Disease, take her to the veterinarian at once.

Wintertime Blues for Indoor and Outdoor Cats

While most people look forward to winter—a joyous time of year complete with a frosty chill in the air, cheerful holiday parties, gathering around a toasty fire, and the aroma of fresh-baked cookies—winter can be extremely stressful and sometimes dangerous for the felines in our lives. During this time of year, you need to be extremely attentive to the special needs of your furry friend. Fortunately, a little preparation and knowledge can help cat owners ensure that this season is a safe and happy one for kitty.

The Warm Feline

Keeping your cat's body temperature regulated should be a main concern during the winter months. Just because felines have a "fur" coat does not mean that they can withstand the blasts of winter air. If you allow your cat to go outside, whether full-time or part-time, you should realize there are certain hazards to watch out for. Felines are small, delicate creatures. During extremely cold conditions, frostbite and hypothermia are as dangerous to your cat as they are to you.

To combat the weather, a comfy cat shelter that is free of drafts must be provided. Place an enclosed bed for

Your feline friend may be happiest when napping on the couch.

Part 3

Frostbite

Areas of a cat least covered by fur are the ones most susceptible to frostbite. The ears, toes, scrotum (in males), and tail are common places for frostbite to occur. Signs of frostbite are easy to spot and include skin that is pale and white, which becomes red and swollen as the cat starts getting warm.

Until you can get your cat to the vet you need to warm the frostbitten areas by immersing them in warm (not hot) water for 20 minutes or until the tissue becomes flushed. Never apply snow or ice. Tissue damage is greatly increased if refreezing follows thawing.

Cats can get frostbite and hypothermia. Limit your cat's outside time during the winter months.

your cat inside the shelter. It should be large enough for her to lie down comfortably in, but small enough to contain the heat generated by her body. A blanket, towel, or sweater on the bottom of the bed will be a welcome sight for kitty to curl up on. Make sure the bed is not sitting directly on the cold floor.

When your cat is frolicking in the snow or simply walking from her shelter to your front door, ice balls can form in between the toes and should be watched for, especially on long-haired cats. Additionally, you should wipe your cat's paw pads off with a damp cloth after she has been outside in case she has walked on any chemicals used to melt ice and snow on the road or sidewalk. Not only can the chemicals irritate kitty's paws, they can also make your cat quite ill if she licks her paws and ingests the poisons.

Winter Woes

One of the most tragic accidents felines experience during the winter months comes from seeking warmth under the hood of a toasty car engine. When you come home from your heated car and go into your heated house, a cold, innocent feline might decide to crawl up inside your car engine to try to get warm. Before starting your car engine, always bang on your car hood, honk the horn several times, and pop the hood to make sure you aren't going to kill or injure a feline taking a long winter's nap.

Part 3

Although freezing temperatures are one hazard winter presents, there are other potential dangers as well. In most areas, the cold weather brings out hunters and trappers. Leg-hold traps with alluring food could tempt any curious feline to investigate further. The results could be deadly. If you suspect there are traps in your area, don't let your beloved cat become fair game. Keep her inside all the time—no exceptions!

As you winterize your vehicles, read the label before putting in that antifreeze. It is a terrible poison, made even more horrible by its apparently sweet, appealing taste. Even a small amount of antifreeze can be lethal to your cat. The good news for pet owners is that there are now non-toxic antifreezes available on the market.

Making Indoors Safe and Sound

Although your cat is definitely much safer indoors during the winter months, there are certain hazards in your home that you should pay careful attention to. Any heat source beckons felines; this includes fireplaces, kerosene heaters, candles, and even your oven. Cold weather usually prompts more cooking and baking, so be especially alert to your cat's whereabouts when using the oven.

Your cats are depending on you to keep them safe, whether indoors or outdoors.

Carbon Monoxide

Carbon monoxide poisoning is just as dangerous to pets as it is to humans. If your cat has been exposed to high levels of carbon monoxide, natural gas, or other types of gas, get her into fresh air as quickly as possible, then call the veterinarian. Installing carbon monoxide detectors in your home and garage will alert you if there is a problem.

If your home has a fireplace or a kerosene heater, protective screens should be in place at all times. To be safe, only use these heat sources when you are home to supervise your heat-seeking cat.

If you are going to be gone from home all day and feel tempted to turn the heat down to save a few dollars, remember the animals in your household count on you to control the elements, including the temperature. Resist the urge to turn that heat down and keep the heat set at a moderate temperature so your cat can rest comfortably while you are away.

There are other winter dangers present in the home that all cat owners need to be aware of. The warm, flickering glow of a holiday candle makes an enticing curiosity to a cat. Often, a cat or kitten will try to "catch" the flame or paw at it, which can result in injury. Even if your cat is trained not to go near a candle, her tail or whiskers may accidentally get a little too close and she could get burned. Never leave a lit candle unattended for any reason, especially if there is a cat in the room.

Winter is a time of gift-giving and present wrapping. As any cat owner knows, felines are fascinated by crinkly wrapping paper and like nothing better than to "help" you wrap a gift by chasing the ribbon. Although your cat may find shiny bows and ribbons fun to play with, you need to be aware that they are dangerous toys for your pet. If your cat accidentally swallows part of a ribbon or bow, she could choke. Keep a close eye on your cat when you're wrapping presents.

Never allow your cat to play with a lit candle. She could get severely burned.

Although bows and ribbons look like fun toys, they are choking hazards. Keep kitty away from them.

Part 3

Christmas trees are beautiful to look at and cats seem to find them particularly interesting. They don't know why the humans have brought a tree indoors, but they are quite willing to help explore what they perceive as their "new toy." Cats like to climb trees and your Christmas tree will be no exception. Be sure to teach your cat to stay away from the Christmas tree, otherwise you may find a whiskered face peeking out at you from one of the top branches.

Christmas trees also make great natural scratching posts. If your cat sneaks under the tree to have a healthy scratch, she may bring the tree down on top of herself. Be sure your cat does not drink the water at the bottom of the Christmas tree. Chemicals are often added to the water to make the tree last longer, and they may make your cat sick. Fallen pine needles can also pose a problem to the curious cat. Your cat may ingest the sharp needles, resulting in injury or illness, or a needle may accidentally get stuck in the cat's paw or eye.

Also be aware of the decorations on the Christmas tree. Shiny glass ornaments make fun toys (or so the cat may think) to swat at, but if the ornament breaks, the broken glass can cause injury to the curious feline. Shiny glitter, tinsel, and garlands are enticing to the average cat, but are also potential choking hazards. If you do decorate with delicate glass ornaments, garlands or tinsel, but sure to place them high enough in the tree so your cat cannot reach them. If you teach your cat to leave the Christmas tree alone, you should have no problems keeping your cat safe around holiday time.

Food for Thought

As in the summer months, your cat's eating habits may change in the winter because cold weather depletes your pet's energy level. In the winter, cats often store more fat because of their decreased activity, but they should be fed the same diet they always get. Be sure your feline gets plenty of exercise to avoid weight gain during these months.

Your holiday feasting may make you feel sorry for kitty as she longingly watches you carve that glistening turkey. It may seem kind to give her a nibble off a turkey leg, but resist the temptation because small bones can splinter, causing internal problems if swallowed. Another food that is bountiful during the holidays is chocolate. For pets, chocolate is a tasty toxin; it contains a compound called theobromine, which, like caffeine, is dangerous to dogs and cats when eaten in large quantities.

Water is a crucial element in your cat's diet. It is important to have fresh water available to your pet at all times. For outdoor pets, frequently check the water dish to ensure ice hasn't formed over the top. Heated water bowls are available in most pet stores if you are unable to regularly check the outside water supply.

The Right Life for Your Cat

As a cat owner, you are responsible for taking care of kitty–whether indoors or outdoors, in the summertime or in the wintertime, and during all situations that may arise for the feline who depends on you to keep her safe.

Keep your cat indoors at all times. She will thank you for keeping her safe.

Obviously, there are far fewer dangers inside your home than outdoors. Even if you have your cat vaccinated for all the communicable diseases (rabies, distemper, feline leukemia) the reality is that the life expectancy for an outdoor cat is almost always a shorter one than for an indoor kitty.

When you adopt a cat and promise to care for her for the rest of her days, you are also promising to guarantee her utmost safety, whether you believe that to be indoors or out. You must, however, look at the situation realistically before deciding where your cat will be safe and secure. But, no matter where your cat spends her days, if you love her enough to do what you believe is best for her ultimate protection and preservation, then she will be free to roam forever inside your heart.

Part 3

13

Keeping Your Feline Healthy

Do you ever wonder how your cat is feeling? Since kitty cannot tell you if she has a headache, backache, if it hurts to go to the bathroom, or even if she's feeling down in the dumps, it is your job, as a caring pet owner, to recognize the physical and emotional signs of a healthy cat. Making sure that your cat is in peak condition begins with knowing immediately when kitty is not feeling her best. Paying close attention to even the smallest change in her eating patterns, bathroom habits, activity levels, and all those other behaviors and quirks that make your furry friend the unique individual she is, will ensure her many years of health and happiness.

Changes in Everyday Routine

Probably one of the most apparent signs that your

Your cat depends on you to keep her in the best of health.

If your cat stops grooming herself, it may be a sign that she is ill.

The Mysterious "Third" Eyelid

Cats have a third eyelid that functions to move tears across the eye and to protect the eye from injury. If this semi-transparent membrane or sheath—also known as a haw—covers a part of kitty's eye, it could be a sign of illness. It should not be evident for any period of time. You need to contact your veterinarian if your cat's third eyelid is exposed on a regular basis.

cat is not feeling quite right is when the normally fastidious feline starts to let herself go…literally. Unkempt fur and a dirty or smelly coat may be one of the first outward signs of illness. Of course, other outward signs such as a runny nose and/or runny eyes, your being able to see the third eyelid, a cough, noticeable scratching, or any other symptom that makes you think your cat does not look quite right should be a warning that kitty may be ill and needs to see a veterinarian.

Another sign that your cat may not be feeling well is a dramatic change in her normal schedule or routine. You probably have a good idea how much your cat usually eats each day, how much water she consumes and, yes, even what "treasures" you will find in kitty's litter box. If any of these habits change (for instance, the water dish is suddenly empty every day or nothing appears in the litter box for a few days), you should recognize the change immediately and call your veterinarian.

Occasionally a cat will skip a day of "movement" without cause for concern. Also, a cat that does not eat for a day, or maybe even two days, is not necessarily ill. Perhaps kitty just has a small upset stomach or is not hungry. Everyone (even animals) goes through periods

Part 3

Signs of Illness

Common signs that indicate your cat could be ill include:

√ Unkempt or dirty fur

√ Runny nose and discharge from the eyes

√ Difficulty urinating

√ Suddenly not using the litter box

√ Haw (third eyelid) exposed

√ Vomiting or diarrhea

√ Not eating for drinking for more than two days

√ Excessive thirst

√ Wheezing or trouble breathing

√ Falling over/loss of balance

√ Cries out in pain when picked up

If you notice any of these symptoms in your cat, contact your veterinarian immediately.

If your cat is acting strange, or her normal behavior has changed, take her to the vet.

of time such as these, but a really sick cat will fast, and you will notice if several days go by without any activity in kitty's food bowl.

If you are not sure about your cat's eating habits, offer her a favorite cat treat and see if she takes the bait. Again, a very ill cat usually will not eat—no matter how tempting you make the food selection. If fasting lasts more than two days, take your cat to see the veterinarian. Of course, if water consumption increases or decreases, this is an even more critical sign that kitty needs immediate medical attention.

Changes in Normal Behavior

Cat owners would probably admit, at one time or another, that their feline friend is "odd" or "weird." But these terms are usually used in a loving or teasing manner. Cats are certainly a species like no other—with their strong independent nature and their mysterious and

If you suspect your cat is sick, take her to the vet right away.

Purring Can Mean Pleasure or Pain

Just because your cat is purring does not mean she is a happy kitty, as most people believe. While it is true that felines will purr contentedly while being petted by their favorite human, they will also purr in other situations. A mother cat will purr while her kittens are nursing. Cats that are frightened or sick sometimes purr. Scientists have yet to determine why and how cats purr, although they believe the sound is produced by a second set of vocal chords in the back of kitty's throat. If your cat is purring without an apparent reason of happiness or contentment, you might want to check with your veterinarian.

almost "cunning" behavior. So, for someone to say that his or her beloved cat is acting strangely actually might seem quite normal.

However, there are two different kinds of strange behavior in felines. One is the normal, everyday, quirky behavior you are used to seeing in your cat. Maybe she sleeps with her paws over both eyes as if playing hide and seek or perhaps she runs through the house at full speed every morning exactly two minutes before your alarm is set to go off. Yes, these behaviors are strange indeed, but to kitty's owner, they are strangely typical.

The type of strange behavior that will alert you that your cat might be sick is the kind of atypical or unusual behavior that your feline does not normally exhibit. For instance, let's say that your cat meets you at the front door every evening without fail when you come home from work. One night you come home and she is nowhere to be found. After a frantic search, you find her hiding in the closet. This might be nothing, but it could indicate a serious problem.

When your cat does something out of character or abnormal, you should make a mental note of it and then continue to watch your cat more than you usually do to check for any other signs or symptoms that something isn't quite right with kitty. Perhaps she is sleeping a lot more than normal, or maybe she is not interested in playing with her favorite toy anymore. Whatever the case, you know in your gut that something is wrong.

Sometimes you have to study all the behaviors, outward and inward, that your cat is displaying before coming to a final conclusion about the wellness (or not-so-wellness) of your cherished companion. No one else knows your cat's bizarre habits or outlandish idiosyncrasies better than you do. Often, you will need to add up all these elements and present them to your veterinarian—along with your "possibly" ill feline.

Never be afraid to follow your instincts if you suspect that your cat might be sick. It would be much better to take kitty to the veterinarian to find out that she is one hundred percent healthy than not to take her and find out later that you should have done so. If you get to know your cat well, then you will certainly be able to tell the difference between a healthy cat and an unhealthy one.

Proper Veterinary Care for Your Cat

Unfortunately, sick cats are not the only ones who need to see the vet. Healthy felines need to see the veterinarian so they remain healthy. This is known as preventive health care. All cats need, at the very least, an annual checkup.

Kitty will need all the necessary vaccinations and a complete physical examination once a year (older cats or cats with special conditions may require more frequent visits). Your cat's doctor should check for parasite infestations, run blood tests, urine/feces cultures, as well as any other tests or special exams he or she thinks the cat needs. Make sure you like and trust your cat's veterinarian so that the three of you can form a long and honest relationship.

Choosing a Vet

Choosing the right veterinarian for your cat is a big responsibility. You shouldn't go to the first vet you find or pick one at random from the phone book. Do your research. The vet you choose will be taking care of your kitty for the rest of her life.

One of the best ways to find a good, reputable vet is to ask other cat owners, friends, and family members to whom they take their cat. Often, someone you

The vet will examine your cat's ears, eyes, and teeth as part of the routine exam.

Ask your vet questions about your cat's health care.

know can recommend a good vet in your local area. When you've found a vet you think you'd like to use, schedule a visit and arrange for a tour of the facilities. The vet's office and examination rooms should be clean and neat. Be sure to observe the staff and see how they interact with the patients and their owners. Do they seem willing to answer questions? Are they patient with difficult pets? Everyone working in the veterinarian's office should treat all the animals gently and with respect.

Take some time to talk to the veterinarian who will be treating your cat. Does he or she own pets? Ask the vet what (if any) veterinary associations he or she belongs to. Does the vet take the time to listen to your concerns about your feline and answer all of the questions you may have? Ask about office hours and procedures for emergency after-hours care. Some veterinarian offices run a 24-hour emergency clinic, others do not.

Overall, get a feel for the vet's office, staff, and of course the vet. Ask yourself if you feel comfortable trusting this person to take care of your cat's health care needs. If you do not feel comfortable, or the veterinarian's office will not allow you to tour the facility, it would be wise to visit another vet in your area. Shop around for the best vet you can find. After all, you'll be trusting your beloved feline to this vet and your cat deserves to have the best care possible.

Doctors Who Make Housecalls

By far, the worst part of taking your cat to see the veterinarian is the long ride (even one mile is too long for most felines) in the car followed by the extremely long wait in the waiting room (and yes, even one minute is too long for most kitties). But there is an alternative—let the veterinarian come to you.

A rising number of pet owners are trying another system of health care for their pets—home veterinary care. As the number of veterinarians who make house calls increases, this low-stress method of medical care for your cat may soon become the standard in veterinary medicine.

The ability to see a cat in her home environment offers a profound medical advantage in treating medical and behavioral problems. When a cat is transported to an unfamiliar, noisy clinic, her normal behavior ceases and she often becomes withdrawn and confused. That is one reason why home health care for cats is such a great idea. You are keeping your animal in her own surroundings and helping your pet feel more at ease–thus helping the veterinarian determine what's actually wrong with your beloved family member.

Kitty Specialists

If a house call veterinarian is not available in your area, there is yet another alternative to taking your cat to the "standard" veterinary practice. "Cats only" veterinary clinics are opening up in more cities and towns each year. These veterinarians, who specialize in diagnosing, handling, and treating felines, have developed a particular interest in working with the mysterious, four-legged, furry creature known as *Felis catus.*

Is it really necessary to take your cat to a veterinarian who specializes in feline health care? Probably not, but it can make quite a difference in your pampered cat's life–both in and out of the doctor's office. Not only is it a more relaxing environment in the reception area (no barking dogs!), but the benefits extend into all areas of your feline's well-being.

One reason cat owners choose to go to a cats-only veterinarian is because someone who treats cats exclusively is going to look at cats differently than someone who treats numerous species. As with any doctor specializing in one area, a cats-only veterinarian is ahead of the game by the sheer volume of experience he or she has with the feline species.

Cats-only doctors are often able to have more specialized equipment than all-purpose clinics. In many cases, costs are lower since the specialized clinic only has to provide equipment and medicine for one species.

In most cases, the veterinarians at cats-only facilities have a special love for felines and maintain their cats-only practices for this very reason. Knowing that your cat's veterinarian has a special place in his or her heart for felines should give you an extra sense of security. The vet most likely has an overwhelming personal, as well as professional, interest in the well-being of all felines.

If you decide to go the route of a cats-only veterinarian, be sure to check the doctor's

Part 3

Veterinarian Membership Organizations

There are many organizations that your veterinarian might have a membership in. Here are a few special veterinary organizations that might sound familiar to you or that your doctor could belong to:

American Association of Feline Practitioners (AAFP)
200 4th Avenue North, Suite 900
Nashville, Tennessee 37219
Phone: (615) 259-7788
Toll-free: (800) 204-3514
Fax: (615) 254-7047
Website: http://www.aafponline.org

American Board of Veterinary Practitioners (ABVP)
200 4th Avenue North, Suite 900
Nashville, TN 37219
Phone: (615) 254-3687
Fax: (615) 254-7047
Website: http://www.abvp.com

American College of Veterinary Preventive Medicine (ACVPM)
3126 Morning Creek
San Antonio, TX 78247
Website: http://www.acvpm.org

American Veterinary Medical Association (AVMA)
1931 North Meacham Road, Suite 100
Schaumburg, IL 60173
Phone: (847) 925-8070
Fax: (847) 925-1329
Website: http://www.avma.org

credentials (which you should do with a "regular" veterinarian as well). The American Association of Feline Practitioners (AAFP), which has been pursuing excellence and continuing education in feline medicine and surgery, boasts an increasing membership of cats-only veterinarians. It is smart to check whether your proposed veterinarian is a member of the AAFP.

Board Certified Veterinarians

The number of board-certified veterinarians specializing in feline health care is growing slowly but surely. The American Board of Veterinary Practitioners (ABVP) has been giving out certifications in feline medicine since 1995. The certification process is not easy but board certification numbers are increasing yearly. A veterinarian does not need to be certified to be a member of the AAFP.

Your veterinarian will play an important role in the life of your pet. Take the time to search for the right doctor for your cat's preventive and overall health care.

Spaying or Neutering Your Cat

When you take your feline friend to the veterinarian you should ask about getting your cat spayed or neutered. At one time, it was the norm to alter any cat at approximately six

Kittens, Kittens, and More Kittens

A fertile female cat can produce up to three litters in a year's time. The average number of kittens born to a mother cat is usually somewhere between four and six per litter. One female cat (and her offspring) can produce approximately 420,000 kittens in only a seven year time period.

A female cat can produce thousands of kittens in her lifetime.

months of age, but, as technology has progressed, more and more experts are agreeing that this simple operation is suitable for younger kittens. This helps control the population explosion because many kittens in shelters and pet stores are already altered before going to their new homes. Your veterinarian should advise you of your options and discuss them with you.

Neutering

The process of neutering a male kitten or cat is a simpler procedure than the spaying of a female and also less expensive. If this operation is performed early enough in a male kitten's life, he will most likely never start the undesirable habit known as spraying. This territorial signal (which has the male backing up and spraying a pungent smelling urine on objects) is a sign to other male cats that this area is already occupied and also serves as a warning that a fight will ensue to capture the attentions of any female in heat in the territory.

Kittens should be spayed or neutered as early as your vet allows.

Part 3

Altering your kitten is a simple procedure and your pet may come home the same day.

Once a male cat has started spraying, having him neutered may not stop the behavior. Cats are creatures of habit and once a certain behavior has started, stopping it becomes a full-time job. Neuter your male before this becomes a problem.

The neutering, or castration, is a simple procedure and poses a minimal risk to the cat undergoing the operation. It may require an overnight stay (according to your veterinarian's policy or according to each individual case) in the animal hospital, but after a few days kitty will be as good as new.

Spaying

As an educated cat owner, you must never fall victim to the thought that you should let your female experience the joys of motherhood at least once in her life. Although a female cat with young kittens usually makes an excellent mother through instinct alone, her attachment to her kittens disappears after they are weaned. Although it seems cold and unfeeling, a mother cat wants nothing to do with her offspring the moment they are ready to fend for themselves. Maternal yearnings and longings are not part of the feline's overall plan.

It is much better (emotionally and physically) to spay your female kitten from the moment your veterinarian gives the word–usually around six to eight months. Don't wait too long because some cats may develop early and surprise you with the news that they are expecting.

Altering a female kitten or cat is a bit more complicated (and slightly more expensive) than the altering of a male cat. Spaying the female involves a small incision in kitty's abdomen for the removal of her reproductive organs. She will be in surgery for less than thirty minutes and then neatly stitched up. Some doctors require their newly-spayed females to spend the night at the animal hospital while others let kitty go home–but only under your watchful eye with the promise to keep activity levels to a minimum.

It is kinder for all concerned, especially in a world of too many adorable kittens and not enough homes, to have your female kitten spayed at the earliest opportunity. She can then spend her time focusing on raising you to be the perfect companion.

The Decision to Vaccinate Your Cat

Vaccinations were something that, at one time, every pet owner was expected to have done for his or her furry friend, and there wasn't any reason not to have a cat get her shots. In recent years, however, there has been some controversy about how safe these annual vaccinations are, including questions about some serious side effects plaguing felines. So, how do you know what is best for your cat? All the vaccines? None of the vaccines?

Your vet will tell you exactly which vaccinations your cat needs.

Sizing Up Your Cat's Needs–The Core Vaccines

Most experts agree that there is no longer a "one-size fits all" approach to vaccinations and that each veterinarian needs to assess each patient for her own individual risks. Overall, vaccines do far more good than harm. But not all patients need all vaccines. Right now, most vets are still giving the three-way combination (Feline Rhinotracheitis, Feline Calici, Feline Panleukopenia) yearly, but some clinics are giving it only every three years.

The American Association of Feline Practitioners (AAFP) and the Academy of Feline Medicine (AFM) lists two types of vaccines–core and non-core. Obviously, the core vaccines are the ones that the AAFP/AFM recommends for all (or most) cats. Probably the most well-known of these core vaccines is the rabies vaccine. The other core vaccines are those included in the three-way combination vaccine, the FRCP.

The Non-Core Vaccines

Risk of exposure is probably the biggest deciding factor when discussing your cat's vaccination needs with your veterinarian. If your cat has no chance of being exposed to a certain illness or disease, then vaccinating against the disease isn't absolutely necessary.

Giving your cat the necessary inoculations will keep her healthy throughout her lifetime.

The non-core vaccines fall into this category. Your cat's veterinarian should discuss all the possible scenarios regarding these non-core vaccines with you.

Perhaps one of the more common vaccinations that some veterinarians suggest their patients skip is the Feline Infectious Peritonitis (FIP), except in very exceptional circumstances (i.e., a breeder experiencing an outbreak). The Bordetella vaccine is not necessary for all cats, and it is best reserved for cats who board frequently or who are show or breeding cats.

Feline Leukemia (FeLV) vaccines should only be given to cats at realistic risk of catching the disease. Many vets give it to all kittens since their lifestyles can change in the years ahead and cats under one year old are at greatest risk of FeLV infection. In subsequent years, your veterinarian may re-evaluate the risk and either decide to continue the FeLV vaccine or stop giving it.

Vaccine-Related Problems

Controversy in the veterinary community continues about the need for annual vaccines. One cause of this controversy is the increase in tumors found at previous vaccination locations on cats. The incidents of this happening are not extremely high, but they are increasing, which causes concern amongst feline experts and cat lovers alike.

In the long run, most veterinarians will tell you that the risks associated with a cat having zero vaccinations or all her vaccinations are clear—the cat who has her vaccines has less of a chance of getting sick. The problem associated with not vaccinating your cat comes from the notion that your cat will never be at risk. Be sure to discuss with your veterinarian, at length, the whys and why nots of each vaccine available for your cat. Agreeing on a suitable vaccination regimen for your furry friend will ensure your feline's long-lasting health and safety as well as your peace of mind.

Common Cat Diseases and Ailments

Your cat can become ill when you least expect it. If you have a multiple cat household, illness and disease can be easily passed along to other cats. That is why vaccinations are so important if your cats are exposed to other cats (or if you sometimes bring in strays or if you foster homeless cats). Although there are numerous illnesses and diseases kitty can acquire, the following is a list of some of the more dangerous ailments that can be spread from cat to cat.

In a multiple cat household, one kitten may pass an illness to another kitten. Vaccinate all pets.

Feline Immunodeficiency Virus (FIV)

This is the disease you may have heard called Feline AIDS. Fortunately, this has no connection with the human version of the AIDS virus but only mimics some of the symptoms, hence the name. As with the human version of AIDS, FIV patients can live with the disease for many years after being diagnosed, as long as kitty is a frequent visitor to the veterinarian. A lowered immune system makes the cat very susceptible to catching other illnesses and diseases.

Currently, there is no vaccine or treatment for FIV. If your cat does have this disease, however, it is important to remember it is not necessarily a death sentence. As long as you keep up with a regular preventative medicine schedule for her, she can live a happy, fulfilled life with her devoted owners by her side. Caring for other FIV positive felines is a way to still be a multiple cat household.

Feline Infectious Peritonitis (FIP)

Although this disease is more commonly found in cats that are frequently exposed to large groups of other felines, as compared to a single kitty in a household, it is quite deadly wherever it hits. Presently, the FIP vaccine is under scrutiny because experts are not sure if it is enough protection against the virus.

This virus's mode of transmission is not definitively known, but the current theory is that it is passed through oral or nasal contact with feces infected with Feline Enteric Corona

To ensure the health of all cats in your home, have them vaccinated against FeLV.

Virus (FECV), a common virus, which then mutates in certain cats to become FIP.

Feline Leukemia Virus (FeLV)

The Feline Leukemia Virus (FeLV) is an illness passed between cats by direct contact. Whenever you adopt a new cat, the first thing you should do is have her tested and then vaccinated against this lethal disease. A wide range of symptoms are possible for a cat that has FeLV including cancerous tumors, anemia, and a weakened immune system. Keeping your cats up-to-date with their vaccinations can help prevent the spread of this vicious virus. However, it is important to stress that FeLV cats can live normal lives and can even live in multi-cat households— as long as the other cats are also positive for FeLV. There are many selfless people who take on the loving parental role and let these cats live out their lives—no matter how many years that may be.

Feline Panleukopenia Virus (FPV)

The Feline Panleukopenia Virus (FPV), more commonly known as Feline Distemper, can leave its deadly virus in the infected environment and can live in the ground for several years. If you have your cats vaccinated against the disease, there is no chance of other kitties contracting it.

A cat that has been infected with the feline panleukopenia virus must see a veterinarian immediately. Symptoms of feline distemper are high fever, withdrawal, vomiting and diarrhea, loss of appetite, and general depression. Many felines, especially kittens, do not survive this illness, but some do live with the help of treatments such as rehydrating the cat (the vomiting and diarrhea usually lead to severe dehydration), blood transfusions (if necessary), and medicines to help control the nausea.

Upper Respiratory Infection (URI)

Your cat seems to have developed a cold. The symptoms include coughing, runny nose and eyes, and excessive sneezing and wheezing, as well as a loss of appetite. These

Urinary Tract Problems

Urinary tract blockage is more common in male cats than in female cats. Frequent urination, straining to urinate, bloody urine, or crying out when trying to urinate are the most common symptoms. If your cat is having problems urinating, take her to the vet as soon as possible.

If your kitten is having trouble using the litter box, take her to the vet at once.

symptoms indicate a much more serious condition than a cold. They are also the signs of an upper respiratory infection (URI), which is especially hard on a kitten.

The infection can be airborne (from coughing and sneezing on another kitten or cat) and is also spread in kitty's saliva and the runny discharge coming from the nose and eyes. The virus can live on a human and be spread by petting an infected cat and then petting an uninfected cat. As with most of the other serious diseases, your cat should be vaccinated against upper respiratory infections so she can live a life without worry of contracting this contagious and damaging illness.

Parasites

Fleas and ticks are the most common parasites to affect cats. Be sure to examine your cat for fleas and ticks every time you groom her, or at least once a week. Indoor cats that have no contact with the outside world run virtually no risk of contacting fleas or ticks.

You may not see the actual flea when you examine your cat. They jump fast and far and may be gone before you can blink an eye. The flea will leave droppings behind, however. Flea droppings are found at the base of the fur and look like flecks of black pepper.

Part 3

Cats that are allowed outside may pick up parasites such as fleas and ticks.

Internal Parasites

Young kittens should be wormed at about four weeks of age. Your vet can test your cat's fecal sample for any internal parasites such as tapeworms, roundworms, hookworms, whipworms, and flukes.

The best way to eliminate the flea problem is to treat the house and the pet. You need to kill the adult fleas and destroy any larvae or eggs that may be hidden in the house (such as in your cat's bed and maybe even your carpet). There are several flea treatments on the market, including foggers, sprays, and powders. Be sure to wash or replace your pet's bedding once the flea problem has been solved to prevent reinfestation.

Your vet can recommend the best treatment for your feline, which may include a flea dip, a collar, powder, or a flea spot applied once a month to the back of the cat's neck.

Ticks attach themselves to your cat and literally suck her blood. In most cases, cats will remove ticks they find on themselves during their regular grooming process, but sometimes the ticks attach themselves in a hard to reach area, such as the base of the neck or on an ear. If you find a tick on your cat, you can remove it yourself; simply grasp the tick with tweezers and pull it gently (but firmly) out of the cat's skin. Apply an antiseptic to the area to prevent any infection and dispose of the tick by flushing it down the toilet or dropping it into rubbing alcohol.

Health and Happiness for Kitty

All devoted cat owners would be extremely grateful if our pets could live illness-free existences. Of course you can cope with the finicky appetites, the middle-of-the-night wake-up calls, the shredded rolls of toilet paper, and even the occasional case of food stolen from your kitchen table, but you cannot cope with a sick kitty. You can, however, try to prevent as many illnesses as possible by making frequent veterinarian visits and keeping a watchful eye on your cat's habits and behaviors.

Although all the things associated with protecting your cat's good health may not seem so crucial when your cat feels great, the less often your cat needs to see her veterinarian, the happier and healthier kitty will be—and feel. Keeping your cat healthy does not have to be an impossible and formidable chore. You owe it to your cat to be her voice when it comes to staying happy and healthy!

Keep your cat healthy and she will be eternally grateful.

In Case of Emergency

Will you be prepared to handle an emergency situation involving your cat? Knowledge of symptoms and treatments could be the difference between saving your cat's life and losing her to an emergency. There are many potential hazards found in and around a typical household, and knowing what to do if your cat has ingested something she shouldn't have, or has met with an accident, can save your pet's life.

This emergency care guide is not a substitute for professional veterinary attention but will give you an idea of the symptoms of many ailments that may befall a cat and what you can do for your pet before you can get to the vet. Immediate veterinary care is a must in the case of an emergency. You should

Would you know how to help your cat in an emergency?

Contacting the Emergency Disaster Hotline

Provided by the American Humane Association, the Emergency Disaster Hotline will be your first point of call in disaster preparedness (including what to do and where to go). Call the following phone number for assistance:

Emergency Disaster Hotline:

1-800-227-4645

They can provide support and disaster relief information.

If you suspect your cat is choking, open her mouth and try to remove the object.

have an emergency phone number readily available for your veterinarian (and, if accessible, a twenty-four hour Animal Emergency Clinic).

Antifreeze Poisoning

Antifreeze poisoning kills many cats each year. Cats drink antifreeze because the smell and taste is so tempting. Never leave antifreeze spills or leaks in areas accessible to your cat. If you suspect your cat has ingested antifreeze, call your veterinarian immediately. He or she may tell you to induce vomiting if the cat is conscious. Symptoms of antifreeze poisoning include wobbling, convulsions, vomiting, depression, and eventual collapse into a coma.

Choking

If your cat is choking on a bone or other object, signs will include retching, salivating, pawing at the mouth, and trouble breathing. Try to reach into the choking animal's mouth and pull out the foreign object. If the airway is obstructed and you can't get at the object, turn the cat upside down and squeeze the abdomen to force the air upwards to dislodge the object (also known as the Heimlich maneuver). If the cat isn't breathing, resuscitate her and get to a vet right away.

Drowning

If you find your cat is in the water struggling or motionless get her out of the water and immediately check her mouth for any foreign debris. Next, hold the cat upside down by her back legs and gently swing her back and forth to drain the water out of her lungs. You may squeeze gently on the chest, but be careful not to use too much pressure or you might injure vital organs.

Part 3

No Bones About It

As small as your cat may look when compared to you, the amazing fact is your little cat has more bones in her body than you do! While humans generally carry 204 bones, your ten-pound tabby is hauling around almost 250 bones.

If your cat appears listless or depressed, a visit to the vet may be required.

If the cat is not breathing, you will have to perform CPR.

Lay the cat on her right side. Pull the tongue partway out of her mouth and close the mouth by sealing the lips together. Blow air into the cat's nose (called mouth-to-nose resuscitation) for three seconds and release until the air comes back out. Repeat these steps until the cat is breathing again. Take the cat to the vet as soon as possible.

Burns

If your cat is unfortunate enough to jump on something hot, such as a gas grill or stove, she will exhibit red, blistered skin around the burned area and the hair might be scorched. Your cat may go into shock. To treat the burn, gently spray or sponge the area with cold water and apply ice packs to the area for fifteen minutes. You may also immerse the burned area in a basin filled with water and ice. On extreme burns, cover the area with a clean, gauze bandage to prevent it from becoming infected.

Second and third degree burns are the most serious types of burns and should be treated by a veterinarian immediately. The vet may prescribe antibiotics and/or recommend a topical solution to ease the cat's discomfort.

Electrocution

Some cats think it's fun to play with and chew on electrical cords. This is a dangerous habit. Be sure your cat does not have access to electrical cords and wires. Cover the cords

Part 3

or tie them up out of the cat's reach. If your cat does fall victim to electrocution, immediately unplug the source of electricity and push your cat away from the cord. If the cat has stopped breathing, you will have to do CPR. Get her to the veterinarian as soon as possible.

Heatstroke

The most common cause of heatstroke is being trapped in an unventilated area, such as a closed-up car. Signs of heatstroke include a rectal temperature of over 105 degrees, extreme panting, weakness, racing pulse, glazed expression, and collapse. If your cat shows signs of heatstroke, immerse kitty in cool water and give her plenty of fluids. An ice pack placed on the inner thighs and around the head will also bring down the body temperature, which should be between 100 and 102.5 degrees Fahrenheit in a normal cat. Take away the ice packs when her temperature returns to normal. Consult your vet to see if the cat should be brought in for a checkup.

A cat that has been exposed to extremely cold temperatures may develop hypothermia.

Hypothermia

Hypothermia occurs when a cat is exposed to extremely cold conditions for an extended period of time. Symptoms for cat owners to look for include: shivering, stumbling, exhaustion, drowsiness, and a low body temperature (80 degrees to 90 degrees Fahrenheit). Place the cat in a warm room and try to raise the cat's temperature by placing her in a warm bath or surrounding her with hot water bottles or heating blankets (carefully used, of course). Try to get the cat to drink warm liquids if she is conscious. Contact your veterinarian immediately for further instructions.

Injuries From Being Caught in a Trap or Car Engine

When a cat suffers a serious injury, she will not be the same cat you know and love. She will be a scared, hurt animal, capable of anything, including biting and scratching her beloved owner. You should never try to pick up an injured pet without securing her first. If your pet is too small to wear a muzzle, you can wrap her head in a pillowcase, towel, or blanket before beginning treatment.

If your cat has been injured in a trap or has been caught in a car engine, there may be broken bones or excessive bleeding. Apply pressure to any bleeding wound and try not to move any bones you suspect may be broken. Your cat will be very scared and in pain, so try to keep her calm and talk to her in a soothing voice. Get the injured feline to a veterinarian or emergency care clinic immediately.

Insect Stings/Snake Bites

Cats, as curious creatures, are likely candidates to be stung or bitten by insects and snakes. If a bee has stung your cat, swelling and hives may occur. The area may be warm to the touch. Your cat may go into shock if she is allergic to whatever stung her.

If a bee has stung the cat, remove the stinger and make a paste out of baking soda and water to apply to the injured area. This will stop the burning and itching. You can also apply a cold compress to the area to reduce swelling. Of course, if your cat has been stung or bitten in the mouth (if, for example, she tried to eat a bee) swelling in the throat could occur and you should take the cat to the veterinarian immediately.

Snake bites are more dangerous but less likely to happen. First, try to identify the type of snake. (It is a good idea to know if there are any poisonous snakes living in your area.) If two fang marks appear side by side on the cat, the bite will more than likely be from a poisonous snake (non-poisonous snake bites will usually leave a horseshoe shaped pattern). Snake bite symptoms from a poisonous snake include pain and swelling, weakness, vomiting and diarrhea, bleeding from the nose and anus, paralysis, convulsions, and coma.

Restrain your cat and apply a tourniquet in the area between the bite and the cat's heart. Loosen the tourniquet slightly so that blood is able to ooze out. You may have to make small parallel cuts (with a sterilized knife) through the fang marks (only about 1/4" deep). Make them up and down if the bite is on the leg. Unless you have an open wound or sore in your mouth, you may attempt to suck the venom out of the wound and spit it out.

If the snake was non-poisonous, clean the wound with soap and water, wipe with alcohol, and keep an ice pack on the bite to stop the swelling. Consult your veterinarian for further instructions.

If your cat goes outside, she may be exposed to lawn chemicals or other toxins.

Poison Control Center Hotline

Because your cat could ingest poison from many sources such as toxic plants, large amounts of chocolate, household chemicals, and many other possible agents, always check with your veterinarian for medical advice or contact the National Animal Poison Control Center at 1-888-426-4435.

In a life and death situation when every minute counts for your cat, dog, or other pet, this 24-hour manned emergency number is your pet lifesaver. There is a fee for this service.

Chemical Poisoning

Even if you use organic remedies on your lawn and garden, your cat might wander into a neighbor's yard and be exposed to harmful poisons. Symptoms of poisoning include vomiting and diarrhea (both of which may be blood-tinged), abdominal pain, lethargy, salivating, convulsions, red areas on the skin (where contact with the poison occurred), weakness, staggering, and eventual collapse.

If you know what chemical poisoned your cat, collect a sample of it. If not, collect a stool or vomit specimen for analysis. Protect yourself from the chemical by wearing gloves when handling the cat if poison is on the cat's coat. (If the cat is covered in poison, rinse her off repeatedly with lots of clean water.) If the poison has been ingested, try to get the cat to drink plenty of water. Depending on the type of poison consumed, vomiting may or may not be induced. Contact a poison control center immediately.

Sunburn

Sunbathing is second nature for a cat. You should be aware, however, that too much sun, especially the scorching summer sun, could cause sunburn, which can lead to skin cancer.

Part 3

Light or white cats seem to have the highest incident of sunburn. Sites of the most common form of sunburn in cats include the ears and/or ear tips. Red, flaky areas develop around the tip of the ear, and there may be a slight curling of the ear tip. Other areas susceptible to sunburn include the nose, the lips, and the eyelids.

You can treat mild sunburn with a veterinarian-approved topical solution. Do not use a sun block designed for humans because the cat will try to lick it off and it could be toxic.

Ensuring Your Cat's Health with Pet Insurance

It is something that every pet owner dreads–your furry friend becomes seriously ill and needs immediate emergency treatment. The emotional stress from worrying about your pet's condition is bad enough, but when you factor in some costly medical bills, the stress on your wallet becomes a concern as well.

According to the American Veterinary Medical Association (AVMA), approximately 58 million American households include a cat or dog. Currently, there are over 52 million dogs and 60 million cats living with families in the US. With that many pets in our lives, there are bound to be medical problems and emergencies. Of course, your animal's health should always be your first and foremost concern, so worrying about how much it is costing to make kitty well again is an unfortunate sidenote during a crisis. Luckily, as the pet population has grown, the concept of insuring pets–just as you do for yourself and your children–is now widely available and accepted.

The American Animal Hospital Association (AAHA) estimates that Americans spend $20 billion annually on their pets. Over 91 percent of pet owners take their dogs and cats to the veterinarian for vaccinations and preventive care. Many pet owners, even the most conscientious, are unaware of the tremendous sophistication of modern-day veterinary medicine.

Medical Costs For Kitty

According to the American Pet Products Manufacturers Association's (APPMA) 2001-2002 National Pet Owners Survey, cat owners say they spend an average of $104.00 per year on veterinary-related expenses.

In the past 25 years, the profession has progressed to the point of offering to

Part 3

Many pet owners purchase pet insurance for their cats.

companion animals virtually all of the modern-day medical 'miracles' enjoyed by humans. Advanced treatment for cancer, high tech diagnostics such as CAT scans and MRI imaging, delicate neurosurgery and microsurgical procedures, and even organ transplantation are a reality in the practice of veterinary medicine today.

Benefits of Pet Insurance

Needless to say, these wonderful, lifesaving procedures can be costly, yet many pet owners want the very best of these services for their pets. The end result, unfortunately, can be a crushing expense that can force an anguished decision between the well-being of the pet and financial hardship. Unfortunately, in some such cases, economic euthanasia or less-than-optimum health care becomes the pet owner's only viable choice. Veterinary insurance for any or all of your pets can be the perfect solution to the possibility that you might be faced with unexpected and expensive medical bills for your cat.

The Bottom Line

The question on most cat owner's minds might be, "Can I afford pet insurance?" There are many reputable companies that offer pet insurance. You should, of course, check with numerous companies and compare costs, coverage, deductibles, etc., just as you would when shopping for your own health insurance. Your veterinarian should be able to give you a list of pet insurance providers.

The increasing value placed upon the household pet as a true family member has never been better understood. The quality and cost of available veterinary medicine have combined to make more

Your feline friend is relying on you to give her the best possible care you can.

Part 3

pet owners aware of their need for affordable protection from large and unexpected veterinary medical costs.

There are many mishaps that could befall your feline. The important thing is to be prepared (physically, emotionally, and financially) and remember to have the appropriate emergency phone numbers of a veterinarian or emergency animal clinic nearby at all times. If your cat does become injured, you will be ready to act with a calm head and provide affordable medical care immediately. Your cat is depending on you!

The Older Cat

Animals age differently than humans. One year of a kitten's life is approximately equivalent to the human age of fifteen. When a cat is seven years old, her age is roughly equivalent to the human age of forty-four. And, when a cat hits the ripe old age of twenty-one in human years, kitty is actually estimated to be about a hundred years old.

A cat that has been on this earth for twelve of our years is approximately sixty-four and is considered a senior citizen. And we all know that senior citizens, of any species, have special needs. For the elderly feline, you need to make sure your pet grows old with dignity, and in the best health possible.

The elderly cat needs extra love and care. This cat is 14 years old.

Cats tend to gain weight as they get older.

Senior or Geriatric Cat?

Have you ever wondered what the difference is between a senior cat and a geriatric cat? For the most part, experts have estimated that at age seven, kitty becomes a senior citizen. At age twelve, however, your furry friend is considered a geriatric cat, which, of course, means even more special treatment for your elderly companion.

Nutritional Needs for the Senior Feline

A senior cat has different nutritional needs than those of kittens or younger cats. Many older cats suffer from kidney problems. While an overabundance of protein is often considered the culprit, experts are not really sure if the two are related. One thing is for certain, though, an older cat who begins having kidney problems should eat a diet low in protein.

If dental care hasn't been a priority up to this point, your cat's teeth could be fairly soft, or even begin to fall out, thus making it hard for her to eat dry food. You can solve this problem by giving her a mixture of quality canned cat food, semi-moist cat food, or by moistening dry cat food with a little water to make it softer for the senior kitty's aging teeth and gums.

Weighty Issues

One problem that befalls elderly cats is that they begin to gain weight. As they age, their metabolism slows down, and often they are not as active as they once were. Excess weight can put pressure on joints and muscles that may already ache from arthritis or other age-related illnesses.

Part 3

Senior Diets

Most cat food manufacturers now make senior formulas. There are many special varieties on the market designed to control specific health issues, such as food designed with a low ash content for cats prone to urinary tract problems, low calorie foods for less-active cats, hairball control formulas, and even dental care formulas. Cats don't readily welcome change in their diets and may become finicky. If you decide to start feeding your cat a "senior formula," be sure to introduce the new food gradually by mixing it with the cat's regular food.

There are many different diets available for older cats.

Older cats do not need as much food as active, younger cats. As long as you feed your senior feline a high quality, nutritional food especially made for older cats, you should be able to control any weight issues. Of course, no matter what age your cat is, clean, fresh water should be available to your cat at all times.

Senior Citizen Exercise

When your cat eventually reaches her retirement years, she will visibly start to slow down and won't be interested in playing or exercising nearly as much as she once was. Because many cats (like humans) develop arthritis and other age-related ailments, it may be painful for your cat to move about and play. However, it is a proven fact that exercising and keeping "limber" actually helps conditions such as arthritis.

You should make sure that you spend time each day trying to get your elderly cat to move around. Don't accept the fact that she will lie in her bed all day, wait to be fed, and then go back to bed. Entice her to run around a bit (although she won't run as fast as she used to) and chase a string or a ball. Any way you can get her interested in exercising is well worth it! Playtime is not just necessary for exercise and energy burning. At all stages of a feline's life, it is also a wonderful way for kitty to bond with her best friend–you.

Part 3

Older cats won't be interested in playing as much as they were when they were young.

Plenty of Water

If your cat is older and you have a large or multi-leveled home, you might want to have bowls of water in several different places in case kitty gets tired and thirsty and can't quite make it down two flights of stairs to get a drink.

Kitty's Retirement Years

With all the advances in veterinary medicine, as well as exceptional care by today's cat owners, the life expectancy of indoor felines is now as high as fifteen to twenty years. A feline will age most rapidly during her first two years of life and then the maturing becomes more moderate through the later years. During your cat's late stage of life, she will need special love and attention from you.

Getting older is not easy for any creature as its physical and mental abilities gradually decline year by year. But you can make your cat's golden years some of the best of her life if you realize your cat is undergoing many changes at this stage.

Physical Changes

Physical deterioration will become more obvious as the aging cat's muscular functions begin to slow down. These bodily changes will, at the same time, probably result in behavioral changes, due to the cat's sense that she is slowly losing control of many areas of her life. The cat might not be able to see and hear as well, and the aging process may alter the elimination habits in some cats.

An aging cat's energy level is probably the most noticeable change in a feline's behavior because the metabolic rate declines at a slow but steady rate over the years. And, although it seems almost impossible that an elderly cat could sleep more hours in a day than a younger cat, she will sleep longer each day. She will tire very easily and may need assistance (such as a stepping stool strategically placed) jumping onto surfaces such as your bed or sofa, which she could do easily once upon a time in her younger days.

Part 3

An older cat's energy level decreases over time. Some cats develop arthritis.

Do Cats Become Senile?

In humans, aging changes in the brain contribute to a loss of memory and alterations in personality commonly referred to as senility. Similar symptoms, such as aimlessly wandering, excessive meowing, apparent disorientation, and avoidance of social interaction, are often witnessed in senior citizen felines.

Arthritis can occur in older cats, especially in cats that injured joints earlier in their life. As in people, arthritis in cats may only cause a slight stiffness, or it can become debilitating. Glucosamine is commonly given to ease arthritis pain and swelling. Remember that cats have a distinct sensitivity (and may have a fatal reaction) to many anti-inflammatory medications such as aspirin and acetaminophen. Do NOT give your cat an anti-inflammatory or pain relief medication unless prescribed by your veterinarian.

As all cat lovers know, cats have a tremendous amount of pride. For the geriatric cat, the inability to jump and play as she once did is probably the hardest thing for her to accept. And, if she misses a jump onto the sofa and falls flat on her behind, it is best if you pretend you did not even notice the mishap. She will proudly pick herself up off the floor and more than likely convince you that she actually meant to miss that jump while practicing her tumbling maneuvers.

Self-Maintenance Matters

When cats get older, they have trouble doing the things they used to do easily and effortlessly. One example is that they do not stretch and exercise their claws as they did

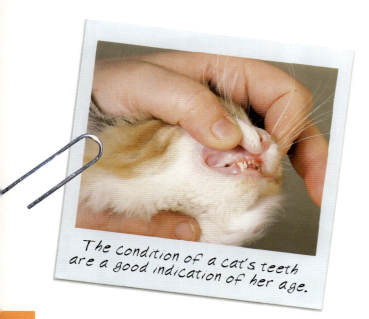

The condition of a cat's teeth are a good indication of her age.

A Cat's Teeth Can Help Determine Age

Examining the teeth is one of the best ways to determine the approximate age of a cat. Look at the degree of growth to determine the ages of kittens, and look at the degree of wear to determine the ages of adult cats. The more wear and tear on the teeth, of course, the older the feline.

Be aware of two things that can throw off your estimate. First, an animal that has received regular dental care will have better-looking teeth than an animal that has not received such treatment. Second, variations exist among animals, even two from the same litter. Teeth are only a rough indicator of any animal's actual age. However, most veterinarians should have enough experience in teeth evaluation to estimate age of any cat whose maturity is in question.

when they were younger. Often, the senior cat cannot sharpen her claws on the scratching posts you have placed throughout your house. Scratching helps to shed the sheaths of the nails, thus preventing ingrown claws. Ingrown claws are a common problem in elderly cats. Regular trimming of your cat's nails (either by your veterinarian, a groomer, or you yourself) will keep this from becoming a serious problem.

Also, your once-fastidious feline may not groom herself as often or as well as she once did. You will need to brush her and keep her general appearance as normal as possible and may have to give her a bath if necessary.

Like humans, felines also suffer from gum diseases such as gingivitis and periodontal disease. Symptoms of periodontal disease in cats include yellow and brown tartar buildup along the gum line, red, inflamed gums, and persistent bad breath. Unfortunately, bacteria

Part 3

Is Surgery Safe For the Elderly Cat?

Growths of various kinds affecting the cat both externally and internally become more common in old age. If surgical treatment is necessary it may still be a realistic option even for very elderly patients. Modern anesthesia allows even the oldest individuals to undergo surgery successfully as long as their basic health is sound. Even a mild degree of kidney or liver damage, or a mild heart problem, would not rule out surgery when it is essential.

Be sure to give your cat extra love and attention as she gets older.

from gum diseases can enter kitty's bloodstream and travel to her major organs. If such infections are not treated in time, they can be fatal.

Senior cats have more incidences of oral disease simply because they've used their teeth for many years. If their teeth were not taken care of properly, they fall victim to the problems associated with the wear and tear of eating and the aging process. If you aren't already taking care of your feline's fangs, start the process today. Take kitty to the veterinarian for a dental checkup and cleaning and learn how to care for her teeth at home to protect that sometimes-ornery/sometimes-sweet smile!

When It's Time to Say Goodbye

Saying goodbye to your feline, especially if you've been together for many years, is one of the most difficult things you will ever have to do. Euthanasia is an option for pet owners who do not want their elderly cats to suffer from the painful complications that sometimes accompany old age. If you need help in making this decision, discuss your concerns with your veterinarian. Most likely, your cat will let you know, in her own way, if and when it is time to make such a decision.

Getting older does not have to be a negative experience if you give your cat proper medical attention and follow a good quality diet regimen. Everything ages; it is part of nature. As long as you treat your aging feline with the care and respect she deserves, getting older can actually mean getting better! Let her enjoy her final years in comfort and peace. It is the least you can do to thank her for all those years of loyalty and companionship.

Feline Behavior Problems

Does your cat ever do things she shouldn't? Does she, for instance, invade your trashcan looking for treasures? Or perhaps she shreds every roll of toilet paper in the house so badly that it looks like a blizzard has blown through your home. Does she like to eat your houseplants? Many cat owners consider all of these actions "naughty" and you may find yourself asking how you can get kitty to behave.

Cats don't misbehave on purpose. They are not trying to annoy you, but are merely acting on their natural instincts. In the wild, these seemingly "bad" behaviors (such as scratching) are part of the cat's daily routine. Your cat needs to learn how to adapt her inherent wild desires to eat

Does your cat misbehave?

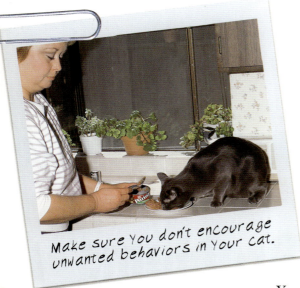

Make sure you don't encourage unwanted behaviors in your cat.

plants and scratch the sofa to the more domesticated setting of your home.

If your cat is "behaving badly" you should ask yourself why. There are several reasons a cat will start to exhibit problem behavior. A common reason is boredom. Do you provide your cat with toys and spend time playing with her every day? Does your cat get enough exercise and stimulation? Sometimes cats will cause havoc as a way of getting your attention. For example, your cat might leap on the table and begin swatting your pen while you're trying to pay the bills. Kitty isn't really interested in your checkbook, she wants you to play with her or pet her for a while. In short, most "bad behaviors" are merely cries for attention from a lonely pet.

Your cat may be doing something "wrong" because of a medical condition. (This is a more serious reason for bad behavior than sheer boredom.) If your cat suddenly stops using the litter box and eliminates elsewhere, it may not be because she doesn't like her cat litter; she may be trying to communicate that she is unwell. Cats that have a urinary tract blockage or infection may urinate outside the litter box or try to "hide" their wastes in other areas of the house. If your cat stops using her litter box, consult your veterinarian. He or she may want you to bring kitty in for a physical.

Cats can become stressed and stress can contribute to problem behaviors. There are many causes of stress: a new human moves into the house, the cat moves to a new house or apartment, another pet in the household passes on, or a new pet is added to the household. A stressed cat may become withdrawn and moody, refuse to eat, or feel the need to "act out" her feelings of insecurity or jealousy. She may defend (or mark) her territory. If your cat is stressed, give her lots of extra attention and love. Treat her gently and talk to her in a soothing voice. Let her know that everything will be fine, and in time, she will calm down and settle into the new circumstances.

Methods of Correcting Your Cat

Correcting a cat should never involve any form of physical punishment. Cats do not understand being slapped or hit and will only respond negatively to punishment of this

Part 3

type. What cats do understand is a squirt of water or a very loud, alarming noise (a hand clap or a firm "No!") when they do something "bad." The hard part is, of course, catching them in the act.

All cat owners should understand that if they come home to find kitty knocked over the garbage can and helped herself to a snack sometime in the past eight hours, squirting her with a blast of water is not going to make much sense now. You have to catch your cat doing the dirty deed; otherwise she will not understand what she has done to deserve the squirt.

Correct your cat's misdeed with a firm "No!"

Whether using the squirt bottle method or the loud noise method, it is crucial to make kitty understand what she has done wrong and the reason for the response. The squirt bottle method requires time and effort on your part. You actually have to catch your cat doing the misdeed and then, if at all possible, squirt her without her seeing you. If your cat realizes you squirt her with water when she is "naughty," then she will soon figure out that these so-called "bad" behaviors are okay except for when you are around to witness them. Feline logic, of course, is different from human logic. Cats are far from dumb and they like to get their own way.

The Urge to Scratch

Kitty has several reasons for scratching and the main reason is to shed the sheaths of the claws so she can grow new claws (just like humans continually grow new fingernails and toenails). Cats have scent glands in their paw pads and scratching any object will mark that particular item as part of their private and personal property.

Encourage good scratching habits in your cat. Give her a scratching post all her own.

A kitten may not be misbehaving on purpose—she could just be curious.

Cats also scratch for exercise purposes. A cat needs to stretch out her legs and feet. A scratching post or kitty condo designed to be scratched and clawed will provide her with the necessary equipment for such exercise. Be sure the scratching post is tall enough for the cat to comfortably stretch her entire body out when sharpening her claws.

Be sure to keep a scratching post close to kitty's favorite sleeping spot because most cats love to stretch out and sharpen their claws when they awaken (however many times per day that may be). Don't be surprised if you find little pieces of kitty's toenails scattered around the scratching post. She is shedding the sheaths of her claws, which is normal.

Teaching Good Scratching Habits

The good news is that furniture scratching is one of the easier of kitty's so-called "bad habits" to break. The more scratching posts you have scattered about, the easier it will be for kitty to fulfill her scratching desires. If possible, provide more than one kind of post for your cat—a cardboard one, a sisal rope one, and a carpet one (only if your cat isn't already a carpet ripper, of course). Your cat will most likely show a strong preference for one type of post and that is the type you should have on hand regularly.

Putting catnip on the scratching post will help attract your cat to it. Encourage your cat to play at the scratching post. If you need to dangle a toy around the post or manually put kitty's paws on the post and show her the scratching motion, then do so. Once your cat learns that the scratching post is hers and hers alone to use as she sees fit, your treasured furniture will have a much longer survival rate. Soon, scratching your beloved belongings will be a distant memory for your furry friend.

If this doesn't work, then you may want to try covering your sofa or chair with a thin sheet of plastic or double-sided tape at the corners or other areas where the cat's been scratching. Cats don't like the feel of these materials on their paws and this may encourage your cat to scratch her post instead.

Part 3

Tail Talking

Feline body language is easy to figure out because cats have several ways of letting their best friend (as well as each other) know their particular frame of mind. Tail talking is one important method of cat communication. Except for the tailless breeds of feline, such as the Manx or Japanese Bobtail, your cat's tail is the primary indicator of mood. Held upright and high, a happy cat's tail is a wonderful sight to see. Coming home after a long day at work, you'll be pleased to see that "happy" tail coming toward you as if to say, "I've missed you and I'm glad you're home."

When your cat swishes her tail back and forth this usually means she is trying to make a decision about what her next move will be. Should she stay on your lap and enjoy getting petted or should she check to see if the food bowl is still empty? Needless to say, cats do a lot of tail swishing. A fast and furiously swishing tail, however, indicates an angry feline, so it's best to leave her alone during this time.

More Naughty Cat Behavior Problems (and Solutions)

Cats are not dumb animals. They can learn and understand things–perhaps not using the same process as human beings do but, nonetheless, they will eventually comprehend what they should and should not do. Some cat owners consider the following behaviors undesirable feline conduct. By recognizing these behaviors and using the correct problem solving techniques, getting your cat companion to stop her "naughty" ways will hopefully be as simple as catching your mischievous kitty taking a well-deserved catnap.

Chewing Electrical Cords

Occasionally a cat will develop a dangerous cord chewing habit. Chewing on electrical cords and wires cannot be allowed because if your feline bites through the cord she may be electrocuted.

Stealing food from the counter is an undesirable behavior. Teach your cat that this is not permitted.

Part 3

Do not let your cat wander on your stove. It is a dangerous habit.

If you catch your cat doing something wrong, correct her right away.

Do everything in your power to prevent cord chewing. Many people put foul-tasting substances, such as Tabasco sauce or Cayenne pepper on their electrical cords. Once kitty takes a taste she'll decide cord chewing is not something she wants to do. You can also tape wires up so they won't be exposed or cover them with a plastic cord cover intended for households with small children.

Jumping on the Counter or Table

If you often leave uncovered food on your counter or table, your hungry and curious cat will probably become a regular visitor. The first rule in preventing this is not to leave any food out. Do not feed your cat scraps in the kitchen while you are preparing dinner or eating at your table. Feeding your cat table scraps will not only encourage the cat to beg, but will give her a taste for (sometimes unhealthy) human food. You do not want your cat to associate food with the kitchen and dining areas.

If your persistent feline still likes to visit your table and countertops, you might want to put something on these surfaces that will startle kitty when she jumps onto them. Empty aluminum cans clanking to the floor or some spoons placed strategically might just scare her enough not to attempt the table and countertop visits again. Cats hate the feel of plastic on their paws, so covering the areas with plastic might deter your curious cat from food and dining zones once and for all.

Of course, the best solution is to train your cat not to go on the counter or table. If you catch her somewhere she shouldn't be, startle her with a squirt gun or make a loud noise to let her know that she is not permitted on these areas. In time, and with consistent reinforcement, your cat will learn the rules of the house.

Plants

If you have poisonous plants in your household you must keep your cat away from them at all costs, otherwise the results can be deadly. But what do you do with your non-poisonous plants? If your cat likes to nibble on your greenery, you have several options. One solution is to move all the plants up high somewhere out of kitty's reach (such as on top of a bookcase or refrigerator) or hang them from ceiling hooks. If you have large, floor-based plants you can put a foul-tasting substance (such as Cayenne pepper) on the leaves and in the dirt around the plant. Once your cat has discovered the plant smells bad and tastes worse, she will not want to investigate further.

Escapes!

How many times have you come home, opened the door, and seen a furry flash zoom by you? Is your cat an escape artist? What can you do to prevent these "break-outs" from becoming a frustrating and dangerous habit?

The most tried and true way of preventing escapes is to have someone hide outside the door and give the cat a squirt of water when she tries to run away. Most likely she will retreat rather quickly. You may also clap your hands loudly or make another sudden sound to startle the cat back indoors.

Most cats like to play with plants. Keep your greenery out of reach.

Some cats are escape artists. Do all you can to keep your cat indoors.

Making Eye "Contact"

A cat's eyes can reveal what kitty is feeling or thinking. The pupils of a feline's eyes can dilate up to five times their normal size when she is frightened or feeling threatened. In normal light, a happy cat should have small pupils that look like little slits in the center of her eye. Eyes that are half closed signify a contented, relaxed, and, (usually) sleepy feline.

A surprised or startled cat will have large, dilated pupils.

If your cat associates spraying water and loud, unpleasant noises with going outside, she soon will be content to stay indoors where it is safe. Also, do your part to prevent escapes. Train your cat to stay away from outside doors. Be aware of your cat's proximity to the door at all times, and if you have lots of guests coming and going, shut your cat in another part of the house until the guests have left.

Garbage Looting

Coming home after a long, hard day only to find your trashcan tipped over and garbage strewn all over the kitchen can make the most understanding of pet owners unhappy. The curiosity of the cat overcomes all reasonable doubts about whether she should or should not be digging in the trash—especially if there are tasty leftovers waiting to be found.

The best way to stop garbage looting and trash tipping is to put the trashcan out of sight and out of reach. Many people keep their trashcans hidden underneath their kitchen sink, which will prevent your pets from garbage looting. If this is not an option, you can purchase trashcans with sturdy lids that snap down, or styles that require you to step down on a hinge to open the can. This will dissuade your "garbage picker" from eating things she shouldn't and making a mess of your kitchen.

Paper Shredding

Have you ever gone into your bathroom and found the roll of toilet paper shredded into millions of pieces of confetti? Some cats think toilet paper makes an excellent toy; it's easy to scratch and it rolls off the tube nicely.

Verbal Communication

Hisses and growls can only mean one thing—your cat is ticked off about something. When this happens, you should retreat and leave your cat alone. When you're simply playing with or petting your furry friend, however, and she growls and/or hisses at you, the best move you can make is a backward one away from the apparent fury of your feline!

Of course, the most familiar verbal sound made by your cat is the "meow" or whatever "word" you hear coming from your feline (such as "mew" or "me-yow"). After spending time with your cat, the various types of "meows" that kitty makes will most likely start to sound distinct, and soon you'll know the difference between her "I'm starving" demands and her "Pet me now" cries!

There are several remedies to this problem, including not letting kitty into the bathroom, putting the paper on the roll so it comes up from underneath instead of over the top (of course, any moderately intelligent feline will soon figure out this trickery and just reverse her rolling techniques), or buying a plastic toilet paper cover.

The Best Solution for Bad Behavior

Sometimes it makes more sense to try to outsmart the cat than to correct her constantly. Finding a suitable alternative works better than fighting and worrying about what your cat is getting into.

Keep in mind that your cat isn't trying to do things wrong on purpose, she may just be curious about the interesting "human" things in the house (especially if she is a young kitten learning all about the world). Your cat may be bored and craving human interaction, especially if she is an only cat. If you do not provide ample entertainment for your cat, she may create her own fun and games, at the expense of your favorite chair.

Almost everything is new and exciting to a kitten. She may not know what is expected of her.

Part 3

Cats will often "misbehave" to get your attention.

With patience and the proper training, you can teach your cat right from wrong.

Be patient when correcting and training your cat, she will need time to learn what is and isn't accepted in your home. By examining the reasons why your cat misbehaves, you will be able to come up with simple solutions to your cat's behavior problems. Almost all "bad" behaviors can be corrected. Take the time to teach your cat right from wrong.

Part Four

General Information

Kitty Classrooms

What to Do With Kitty When You Travel

Whether you are going on a ten-day business trip or a quick weekend retreat to your favorite resort, you will not be able to have a good time if you are worried about your cherished cat. Whether she is locked up in the bathroom of your rented villa, at your house being cared for by a professional pet sitter, home alone (with a friend or neighbor frequently looking in on her), or at a boarding facility, you should be aware of all the alternatives for kitty before you make travel plans.

A Travel Companion

Of course, when you are considering traveling to an exotic locale for a pleasure trip, your first visions might include your cat curled up beside you in front of a roaring fire or stretched lazily beside you under

Would your cat make a good travel companion?

Some cats like to travel with their owners.

If you and your cat are staying in someone else's home, be sure kitty obeys the rules of the household.

an umbrella on a tropical beach. But is it reasonable to expect your cat to travel with you on your vacations?

Some pets (particularly dogs) can be excellent traveling companions. It stands to reason that if you accustom your pet to travel at an early age, she will adapt to it more quickly. For cats, early learning is very important. The things you teach a kitten in those first weeks and months will stay with her for a lifetime. If you take your kitten with you on frequent car trips you will teach her just how much fun traveling can be when the two of you are together on the open road.

[P]etiquette When you are a Houseguest

Often when traveling, you may find yourself a guest in someone else's home. What should you do if you want to bring your cherished feline companion along to your gracious host's dwelling? Is there a proper way to handle such a situation?

You must ask your host about the possibility of bringing your cat with you during your visit and explain that you will take full responsibility for your pet's care during the stay. If your cat is welcomed into the home as an additional guest, you must be sure you follow certain "[p]etiquette" rules to ensure a safe, happy, and stress-free visit for everyone involved.

Where should your feline spend her time? She should be kept in a quiet place of her own. Introducing cats successfully takes weeks, so a guest should not expect that her cat will immediately get along with the host's cat, and the two cats should not be thrown together. If your stay is an extended one, perhaps then, and only then, should you let kitty free to roam—and that is only with your host's approval, of course. If the hostess does not have pets of her own, or if she is not accustomed to having a cat underfoot, your cat might escape accidentally. So there is nothing wrong with leaving kitty in your sleeping quarters behind closed doors. She'll probably feel much safer there.

Keeping Kitty's Routine

Cats love routine and, obviously, taking kitty out of her home is certainly going to cause a change in that routine. It is essential, however, to keep things as normal as possible once you arrive in your guest accommodations. You should bring all of your cat's necessities such as her food, bowls, toys, scratching post, bed or blanket, and even her brand of kitty litter with you.

Give kitty a place of her own to sleep when you travel.

You might want to try disposable litter boxes so as not to have to carry a used litter box with you on the return trip, or throw away a good box before leaving. Bring the same litter your cat uses at home, a scoop, and your plastic bags. If your host has a cat, using your host's scoop will introduce unfamiliar smells into the litter of your cat and that of your host's cat, which could cause litter box problems. Even something as seemingly

Flying With Your Cat

If you do take your pet traveling with you, be aware that airlines may have restrictions on flying with pets. Some airlines may allow you to bring your cat on the plane with you in an approved cat carrier, provided the cat carrier can fit under your seat. Other airlines may require you to "check" your pet in and it will ride in another part of the plane. Call your airline and discuss their pet policy before you make final travel arrangements.

Think about whether you want to put your cat through the stress of flying and being separated from you for long periods of time in unfamiliar, noisy environments. Would your cat be happier if she were left behind in the care of a family member or neighbor?

Part 4

Be sure to bring your cat's food, litter box, and toys with you when you travel.

If you are staying at a friend's house, spend extra time with your cat so she knows she's loved.

inconsequential as sharing a litter scoop could cause your cat, as well as your host's cat, to stop using the litter box altogether–that could certainly put a damper on the entire trip!

Leave your cat's carrier or crate open for her to retreat into because she will probably feel comfortable in there after traveling in it to get to your destination. It is also smart to leave one of your previously worn sweatshirts for kitty to sleep on; it will help calm her down should she feel scared or alone.

Spending time with your feline at a friend's or relative's house is possible as long as you realize it's your responsibility to keep your cat safe, happy, and out of trouble! Be sure to spend some quality time with kitty because, in these unfamiliar surroundings, she will need your love and support all the more.

It takes a special cat, however, to actually enjoy traveling. Cats are creatures of habit. While a change of scenery might seem exciting, you, as a responsible cat owner, should think long and hard about where your cat would be happiest. If traveling across the country, or perhaps even halfway around the world, with your cat leaves any doubts about her willingness to participate, you should consider other arrangements for kitty while you are off on your dream vacation or business trip.

Find a Friend Willing to Kitty-sit

Finding a trusted friend willing to take your cat or cats into their home during your absence has its pros and cons. If you are going to be gone for an extended period of time, you wouldn't have to worry about inconveniencing a friend who will have to go to your

Foreign Travel and Pets

If you are traveling to a foreign country for vacation, you might not be allowed to bring your cat into the country for various health reasons. Customs regulations may require your cat to remain in quarantine anywhere from several weeks to several months. Be sure to investigate the rules and regulations of traveling with a pet with your travel agent. He or she may advise you to leave your pet at home.

Some cats do not enjoy leaving home and may become stressed.

house (one or more times per day) because kitty would already be in a home and be monitored. Plus, living in a home with other people and possibly other pets will keep your cat from becoming dreadfully bored. It would be best if your cat knows the person or family she is living with so the change won't be too traumatic.

The downside of this, however, is that changes of scenery might be too stressful for an especially sensitive feline. Being around other pets (if this is the case), could cause problems such as fighting or contracting an illness. Perhaps the worst-case scenario, however, is something that happens when a pet stays in an unfamiliar home–the escape.

No matter how careful someone is, a pet can slip out the door in a fraction of a second. And, unfortunately, your friend may not be as careful about leaving doors or windows open as you are. If your cat escapes from your house, she usually will find her way back or not stray far. But when any animal is in a strange place, it won't recognize the sights, sounds, and smells of "home" and may wander off without being able to find its way back. A lot of pets disappear under these circumstances, so perhaps the best way to avoid such a tragedy is not to send kitty away from what she knows.

Part 4

Jacobsen's Organ

Did you know that cats can smell with their mouths as well as their noses? A small organ located on the roof of the mouth, behind the front teeth, can detect airborne aromas in a manner similar to the nose sniffing out smells. This sensory tool, commonly called Jacobsen's organ, is a small tubular opening, measuring about half an inch in length, and is highly sensitive to chemical smells, such as the pungent odor of urine which is emitted by other felines.

When this organ kicks in, (known as the Flehmen response) kitty makes a peculiar face as her mouth opens slightly and the airborne materials take hold of the cat's senses. Incidentally, traces of a similar organ can be found in humans but, due to evolution and the strong visual sense man has acquired, it is believed to have slowly disappeared because of it was not of use to us.

Your cat might be happiest if she is left home alone in familiar surroundings.

Staying Home Alone

One other alternative when deciding what to do with kitty while you travel is probably your feline's favored option of all— leave kitty home! Letting your cat stay in her own environment is the nicest thing you can do for her. As long as you make the necessary preparations, you can feel secure in knowing your cat is lounging on her special chair while looking out her favorite window and dreaming of your return. Ask a friend to stop in once a day or every other day to check on your pet. Cats can be left alone for a few days at a stretch. If you have multiple cats in your home they will keep each other company. Leave plenty of toys out so kitty can play when she feels the urge.

Leave a detailed list of written instructions, no matter how competent your kitty's caretaker is. Don't assume the person knows anything. List the amount of food and water to give, brand of food you prefer to feed, name and dose of any medications the cat needs, and your phone number.

Another important piece of information you need to leave (where your caretaker can easily find it) is the phone number of your veterinarian in case your cat requires emergency care while you're away. It might be wise to sign a Pet Care Authorization as well. The named

Alert Firemen to Pets Inside

Whether you are on vacation or at the grocery store, a tragic event can happen anytime. In the case of fire in your home, your most prized possessions are other family members and your pets. You can purchase signs that let you write in the number of cats and/or dogs currently living in your home and post them where firemen and police can see them and will be able to rescue your furry friends.

Cats generally sleep between 18 and 20 hours a day. Kitty might not even realize you've been gone!

caretaker(s) should have the power to seek and authorize appropriate medical treatment for your cat(s) in case of an emergency.

One of the most crucial things you can do for kitty is make sure she has the proper identification. Be sure your cat wears a collar and identification tag at all times. Both outdoor and indoor cats need some way of being identified if they are lost or injured. In spite of everyone's best intentions, an indoor cat occasionally gets out. Be sure to put your veterinarian's or a friend's phone number on the tag in addition to your own. If you are on vacation, no one will be able to reach you at your home phone number.

Hire a Pet Sitter

If you don't want to take kitty with you and you don't know anyone trustworthy who will look after your pet, you should consider hiring a professional pet sitter. Of course, it is always better for kitty to actually know and feel comfortable with the person who will be caring for her in your absence. If that isn't possible, a pet sitter with references and a business that is bonded or insured is a viable solution to your problem.

Pet sitters care for your pet in your home. They either stay or stop by daily (or several times a day) to take care of your pet. There are several organizations you can contact to find pet sitters in your area such as the National Association of Professional Pet Sitters or

Part 4

A cat left alone for days on end can get very lonely.

Oh, So Lonely Without You

Proper food, water, temperature conditions, and other physical needs are crucial in caring for a cat. However, emotional needs are just as important because a lonely cat can be a destructive cat. If you travel a lot you should have more than one pet. An only cat can really suffer when her owner is away, even with a good sitter coming in. A little an mal all alone in a house or apartment, day after day, night after night, can become very anxious. This is one of the most persuasive reasons there is for having at least two cats!

US Kennel Statistics

According to the National Association of Professional Pet Sitters, 60% of households in the US have pets, and there are 110 million cats and dogs we call family members. But whether they are furry, feathered, or covered in scales, we love our pets and invest heavily in their care. Statistics show there are 9,000 boarding kennels in the US serving approximately 30 million pet owners annually.

Pet Sitters International. If your pet sitter is a member of one of these professional organizations, you can feel safer entrusting the care of one (or more) of your dearest family members to him or her.

Kennels and Boarding Facilities

Although there are numerous choices for kitty when you travel, boarding her in a kennel-like setting is a very popular choice among cat owners. Finding a high-quality boarding facility, however, is essential so you should do a lot of checking, asking around, and visiting area kennels before entrusting your best friend's happiness and well-being to a stranger.

Of course, after considering all your options—including hiring a professional pet sitter, having a friend or neighbor stop in your home, taking your pet with you, or even letting kitty stay in a relative's or friend's home—boarding your cat might be your best choice.

Part 4

Finding a Pet Sitter In Your Area

You can contact the following organizations to find a pet sitter in your area:

National Association of Professional Pet Sitters (NAPPS)

17000 Commerce Parkway

Suite C

Mt. Laurel, NJ 08054

Phone: (856) 439-0324

Fax: (856) 439-0525

Website: http://www.petsitters.org

Pet Sitters International (PSI)

201 East King Street

King, NC 27021

Phone: (336) 983-9222

Website: http://www.petsit.com

Make sure you're leaving your pet in good hands. Check the references of any pet sitter.

Searching for a Kennel

When you hear the word "kennel," you might think of small, steel cages with barking dogs, hissing cats and an unhappy pet population waiting for their beloved owners to rescue them. The kennels of today, however, are much more advanced and extremely personalized.

One reason why modern boarding kennels are safer places to leave pets is because stricter laws are being passed (and enforced) so these

How to Contact the American Boarding Kennels Association (ABKA)

To locate ABKA-certified kennels in your area, you can contact them at:

American Boarding Kennels Association (ABKA)

1702 East Pikes Peak Avenue
Colorado Springs, CO 80909
Phone: (719) 667-1600
Fax: (719) 667-0116
Website: http://www.abka.com

Part 4

Modern kennels provide large, roomy cages for pets.

Your cat may anxiously await your return if you've been gone for several days.

businesses are being monitored, for the most part, by local law enforcement officials. There are nationally run organizations, such as the American Boarding Kennels Association (ABKA), that you can contact to check out specific kennels and see if they are members of such associations (which means the kennel would have to live up to certain criteria). The Better Business Bureau can let you know if the kennel you are considering has ever had any complaints filed against it.

One place that often will board your cat (for a fee) is your veterinarian's office or another local veterinary clinic that has its own boarding facility in conjunction with the clinic. While this may seem like the perfect place to leave kitty–if your cat gets sick, she'll have a doctor in the house–it might actually be a bad idea because many animals associate the veterinarian's office with "unpleasant" times. Since you want your pet to be as comfortable and unstressed as possible during your absence, you might want to think twice about kitty staying at the same place she has to go whenever she is sick, needs vaccinations, or other medical procedures.

Inns and Hotels for Cats

When shopping for temporary accommodations for your feline friend, you might imagine spacious suites with plenty of catnip, toys, and personal attention. Yes, this is the updated version of yesterday's cat kennels. Hotels, inns, and even bed & breakfasts for kitty are the latest rage among traveling cat owners. In fact, some of the places you can book your cat into just might be nicer than where you end up staying during your time away!

Worrying about your cat while you're on vacation is the last thing you want to do. That's why the concept of hotels, spas, inns, and bed and breakfasts specifically designed for felines is quickly rising in popularity. Knowing kitty is in a luxurious hotel room, being played with, brushed, fed, petted, and consistently monitored, will make your time away less stressful and more enjoyable.

Many of these new hotels and inns include guest rooms of differing sizes to accommodate one cat or a family of multiple cats who are used to being together. Besides the minimal requirement of feeding and medicating cats, these feline resorts cater to kitty's every whim and include grooming time and even play time to avoid boredom and relieve the stress associated with being in an unusual place. There is a wide range of accommodations out there, so be sure to check out all the options.

Inns and hotels designed for cats make them feel like they're at home.

Welcome to the Inn

There are so many inns and hotels for felines cropping up around the country that it would be almost impossible to keep up with the list of such accommodations. So, from coast to coast, here are a few cats-only luxury spots to reserve for your pampered cat.

Catnap Inn
Virginia Hughes, Owner
3530 Lincolnway West
South Bend, IN 46628
Phone: (219) 288-7877
Toll Free: (866) 673-9436
Website: http://www.catnap-inn.com

The Country Kitty B & B
Kip and Jean Grant, Owners
1195 Ridge Road
Queensbury, NY 12804
Phone: (518) 792-6369
Website: http://www.countrykitty.com

Kitty Hill Resort for Cats
Harriet Butts, Owner
126 Vernon Street
Santa Cruz, CA 95060
Phone: (831) 427-2287
Website: http://www.kittyhillresort.com

Part 4

Check references and pay a visit to the kennel you are considering using.

Choosing a First-Rate Facility

One of the main things you should look for in a boarding facility is the level of cleanliness. Everything touched by someone else's cat should be disinfected and cleaned before a new guest arrives. All reputable boarding facilities require proof of current vaccinations to prevent the spread of any diseases or illnesses, even though cats from different households may never come in contact with one another.

Keeping track of your cat's food intake and bathroom habits should be a priority with the employees of the boarding facility you choose. When cats are very stressed, they may go one or even two days without eating but cannot go without drinking. A responsible kennel owner will have a signed authorization from you to take kitty to a veterinarian in case of an emergency situation, or if your cat refuses to eat or drink for too long a period of time. Transporting kitty to a veterinarian should be one of the services available at any reputable inn, hotel, or kennel.

By most standards, cats are probably a lot easier to care for in a kennel setting than dogs are simply because they sleep most of the time (12 to 20 hours per day) and don't need a lot of exercise. Also, because they are not "pack animals," like dogs are, cats really do not need the company of other animals nor do they require separate exercise areas. Felines are pretty much content when housed in roomy primary enclosures.

Reunited and Ready to Go Home

Finally, when the time comes and you get to reunite with your cat and go "home sweet home," you should ask a few questions about how your cat fared during her stay at the facility. Did your pet adapt well to kennel food (unless you brought your own, of course), the routine, and overall environment? Did she display any unusual behavior or require any special handling?

This information should be entered into the kennel's records to assist kennel personnel in

Part 4

caring for your pet during her next stay (if needed). But you should also be aware of your cat's experiences during her stay in the event that you move away from the area or choose to use the services of another kennel in the future. Hopefully, that won't be for quite a while because, whether she would ever admit it or not, your cat surely missed her familiar surroundings, her own bed, and you, her best human friend in the world.

If you can find a capable and willing person to look in on your pets while you are away, it truly will be a relaxing time for all, including your feline friends. So, whether you're planning your annual vacation or a last minute business trip, remember to consider all the options for your cat. Everyone will have a relaxing and enjoyable vacation, whether it's on a tropical island devouring fresh tuna or lazily catnapping on a fluffy pillow at home.

Your cat will be happy to see you and even happier to go home!

Part 4

Showing Off Your Cat

Have you ever been to a cat show and witnessed all the beautiful breeds of felines strutting their stuff for everyone, including the judges, to see? You may secretly wish to become part of the glamour and excitement but might not be sure how to get involved in this world known as the Cat Fancy. It isn't as mysterious as it may seem, and no matter what type of cat you own, it can be one of the most rewarding experiences of your (and your cat's) life.

Do you have a pedigreed, registered cat, or do you have a mixed breed cat? The good news is that you can show either. Most associations divide cats up into four categories: Kittens, Championship, Premiership, and Household Pets (HHPs).

Cat shows are popular events with thousands of feline fanciers.

Pedigreed cats, like the Russian Blue, can be entered into many different categories.

Cat Show Categories

Kittens

Pedigreed kittens aged four months to eight months. In some associations, kittens do not have to have an individual registration number to be shown, but their litter must be registered with the sponsoring association. Kittens may be spayed or neutered.

Championship

Pedigreed, registered, unaltered cats over eight months old. This class tends to be the largest and the most competitive.

Premiership

Pedigreed, registered, altered cats over eight months old. Premiers are not cats who were not "good enough" to breed. Many catteries alter top males to show in premiership because of the difficulty of keeping an intact male. There tend to be more neuters than spays, although there are some spays as well.

Part 4

Many cats in Premiership, particularly older ones, are cats that have been retired from successful breeding programs and have had success in Championship class. Premiership is still a great way to promote a cattery, further interest in a breeding program, and have fun showing an excellent animal. In some associations, such as The International Cat Association (TICA), premier entries may be declawed. The Cat Fanciers' Association (CFA) does not allow declawing.

Household Pet (HHP)

Altered, usually mixed-breed cats of known or unknown heritage. In some associations such as TICA, HHPs may be declawed. The CFA does not allow declawing under any circumstances.

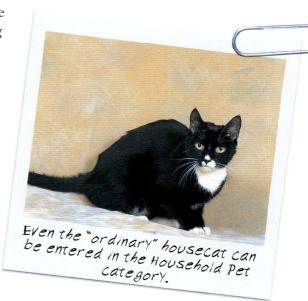

Even the "ordinary" housecat can be entered in the Household Pet category.

Finding the Right Registry

Before you register your cat with an association, you should know there are several possibilities and you can register your purebred with more than one of these registries.

Should You Breed Your Cat?

To breed or not to breed? This is a question many cat owners have asked themselves at one point or another. The answer, however, is very simple—unless you are a qualified, professional breeder who already has homes for all the kittens to be born—you should not even think about breeding your cat. With the continuously exploding population of unwanted, homeless felines, there is rarely a viable reason to allow your cat to breed.

Preparing For Showtime

Preparing your cat properly before a show is crucial. Be sure your cat gets a good balanced diet and exercise. If you have the opportunity, get your cat used to being handled by strangers. If kitty hasn't had her shots, be sure to get them. It is imperative for your cat's health (and the health of the competition) that all routine feline vaccinations be up to date. Try to get this done a few weeks ahead of time to allow for any unexpected reactions to pass.

Part 4

Judges of pedigreed cats check to make sure the cat follows the written standard for the breed.

A regal Burmese can capture the attention of the cat show judges.

CFA

The biggest registry in the world, as well as the most widely known is the Cat Fanciers' Association (CFA). Started in 1906, to date it has registered over one million felines. The benefits of registering your pedigreed cat with this association are many, the greatest being its world-renowned recognition. CFA also established the Winn Feline Foundation, a foundation which funds research and studies in developing exceptional feline health.

ACFA

Known as the association of "firsts," the American Cat Fanciers Association (ACFA), founded in 1955, was the first association to hold double, triple, and quadruple championship and grand championship rings. ACFA was also the first registry to accept altered cats for championship competition (against other altered cats, of course). They were also the first association to require prospective judges to complete written exams before being licensed.

TICA

The International Cat Association, Inc. (TICA) is the world's biggest genetic registry of pedigree and household cats. TICA, formed in 1979, adopted a judging format that doesn't mention status, title, or identification of show entries. Cats are judged entirely on their merits at the time of judging.

CFF

The Cat Fanciers' Federation (CFF) was organized in 1919 and today its shows often benefit animal welfare organizations and humane societies. CFF was the first association to allow breeds not currently recognized for competition in the Any Other Variety (AOV) division. CFF oversees cat shows, keeps ancestry records, and trains judges to abide by and uphold CFF ethics.

ACA

The American Cat Association (ACA) is the oldest cat registry in the US and was started in Chicago in 1899. The ACA's goals are to support pedigreed cats as well as their owners by overseeing cat shows and maintaining a studbook registry.

CCA

In 1961, the first Canadian cat registry, the Canadian Cat Association (CCA), was born. Until that time, Canadian cat fanciers had to register their purebreds with American or European associations. Today, CCA boasts over 110,000 registered felines and accepts household and altered cats as well as the pedigreed.

GCCF

Four years after CFA was formed in the US, England formed its first cat registry. It is called the Governing Council of the Cat Fancy (GCCF).

FIFe

The largest European cat sanctioning body is the Feline International Federation (FIFe), which includes many countries in Europe, Asia, South America, and Australia.

Advantages of the Household Pet Category

In some ways, showing a HHP is easier and less stressful than showing a pedigreed cat. HHPs compete strictly on beauty, health, and temperament. They don't have a written standard. The HHP class tends to be more relaxed and a lot of fun. In short, you don't have to be a breeder to show beautiful cats in the HHP competition.

Make sure you groom your cat before you show her. You want her to look as pretty as possible.

Some cats become stressed from the show excitement, while others thrive on the attention.

Part 4

A household pet will be judged on her beauty and grace.

Judging the Household Pet Category

In the Household Pet category, the standards for judging are very broad. Basically, the judge is looking for a "nice cat."

√ Is the coat clean?

√ Does kitty have fleas or other parasites?

√ Are the corners of the eyes clean?

√ Are the ears clean inside?

√ Is the cat a good weight for her size, or is she overweight or scrawny?

√ How does she handle?

√ Is the cat purring, or scared or somewhere in between?

√ Is the cat beautiful?

√ Does she have some unusual markings?

As long as she doesn't "maul" the judge and has a pleasant disposition, she will most likely do fine.

Is My Cat Show Material?

In the HHP category, cats are judged not on a specific standard but on their beauty, personality, condition, and balance and proportion. Temperament is as important as clean, well-groomed fur, a good physical condition, and an attractive appearance. How the cat reacts to being judged can influence a judge's decision.

A mixed breed cat will do well if she's comfortable around strangers and takes things calmly. A cat with self-confidence and poise will do better in the show ring than a cat that jumps at every shadow. You can test your cat's show potential by having a person with whom the cat is not familiar with come over and do a mock judging. Have the person place the cat on a table, stroke her, run a hand through her fur, and wave a feather in front of her face. If kitty freaks, then a show cat she is not!

Part 4

Rules and Regulations

All of the feline registry associations have slightly different guidelines, and you will need to check the specific rules for the cat show in which you intend to enter your feline. Normally, in the household pet division, all the cats are judged together, despite age, color, coat-length, or gender. This differs from the purebred categories, classifications, and groups—which can be confusing to the cat show newcomer. Luckily, the household pet competition is fairly simple to understand.

Most of the registries (but again, each will have a different set of rules) state that cats over a certain age must be neutered or spayed. This is a great rule because it is a positive way to help control the feline overpopulation problem. Also, many of the registries insist the cats not be declawed. This is a responsible way to stop the needless amputations of thousands of kitty claws.

The Secret of Kitty's Success

Is there a secret in owning a successful HHP show cat? The answer depends upon your definition of success. Anyone can be considered successful without coming home with a ribbon. If you've enjoyed yourself, grown closer to your cat, learned from the experience, advanced the feline cause, met like-minded people, and had fun, the show was a success regardless of the outcome.

If Kitty Has an "Off" Day

Your cat needs positive reinforcement. Never punish a cat for behaving badly in the ring or if she does not place as high as you would expect. In fact, an extra hug and treats may be in order. You need to make the show fun for your cat—punishing her will only make her hate competing in cat shows. Unfortunately, some exhibitors may display anger toward their cats if they do not win, or if the cat behaves badly in the ring. Showing is not for every cat. Some just do not have the basic temperament. Even a great show cat with lots of experience can, regrettably, have an off day.

Entering cat shows is a fun and rewarding hobby for people of all ages.

Part 4

Feline Lore

The cat. Aloof. Mysterious. Independent. And, of course, exceptional…

As far as we know, the ancient Egyptians were the first people to realize the exceptional value of the cat and they worshipped them. Thousands of years ago, if you happened to be lucky enough to be a cat in Egypt, you lived an extremely good life. You would be treated better than a king or queen, as ancient Egyptians believed cats were more important than kings and queens…cats were goddesses!

Independent and Worshipped

A temple was erected to worship the cat goddess of femininity and fertility, Bast. There was an annual

Cats were worshipped in ancient Egypt. Some still are today!

Cats such as the Egyptian Mau were held in high regard in ancient societies.

Cats Who Hold Their Tails High

Of all species of cats, the domestic cat is the only one able to hold its tail vertically while walking. Wild cats hold their tails horizontally or tucked between their legs while walking.

festival to celebrate Bast in which hundreds of thousands of people traveled to the city of Bubastis, where the temple that housed the sacred statue of Bast was located. If you killed a cat in Egypt during this period, it was considered a capital crime and you were severely punished.

On one known occasion, a mob lynched a Roman soldier who had killed a precious Egyptian cat. Losing a cherished cat companion in ancient Egypt would prompt the entire family to shave off their eyebrows in mourning for the immense loss of their sacred pet.

Thousands upon thousands of Egyptian cats were mummified after death, which is another indication that they were highly valued. The cats' owners often placed a saucer of milk and mummified rats and mice in the cats' tombs. Since pharaohs were mummified as well, it only proves that cats were held in the same regard as these royal leaders.

History books tell the story of the independent cat being domesticated mainly for her ability to hunt the granary-ravaging rats. These creatures, however, have meant so much more to humans than simply acting as rodent control. Kitty's aloofness, though, might have something to do with what happened after those centuries of Egyptian worship.

Part 4

Independent and Prosecuted

If you were unlucky enough to be a feline or, even worse, a black feline, during the Middle Ages yours was most likely a life of oppression and abomination. The people of this time period not only hated the cat but also feared its supposed mysterious and cunning ways.

During this time period, thousands of innocent cats were tortured, burned at the stake, or killed on sight. The mass extermination of the cat was so great that the population of cats living in Europe diminished to less than ten percent of its original number.

There was a brief pause in cat killings during the years of the Black Death. With hundreds of thousands of people dying from this fatal illness, the Europeans had neither the time nor the energy to continue the persecution of the cat.

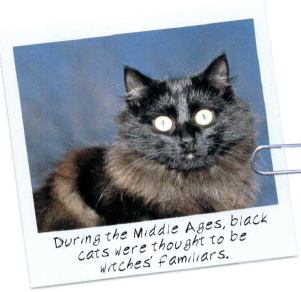

During the Middle Ages, black cats were thought to be witches' familiars.

Big Cats or Little People?

Cats do not think they are little people. Instead, they believe humans are big cats. Obviously, this influences their behavior in many ways.

Your cat will consider herself one of the family.

Part 4

No matter what pattern or color the cat appears to be, all cats have "tabby" genes.

Why Are Felines Referred to as "Tabby" Cats?

Many people refer to cats in general as "tabby" cats. Although that may seem to be an error when looking at a solid black, tortoiseshell, or cream and white feline, it is actually a correct term, genetically speaking. Tabby is a pattern rather than a color and, no matter what color or markings are apparent on kitty; all felines have the tabby genes in their genetic makeup. However, other color and pattern traits may hide those tabby markings, therefore making them dormant in many types of cats.

The cat responded to this absence of persecution by multiplying and attacking the plentiful food supply around them, those tasty, plague-carrying rats. We, of course, promptly rewarded the brave kitty for helping to save mankind by resuming the feline inquisition right where it left off.

In Europe, if you happened to be an "independent" elderly woman who liked cats, you had a very good chance of being suspected of witchcraft. Somewhere between half a million and one million people died as a result of the witchcraft trials. Unfortunately, many more innocent felines were murdered right along with them. This thousand-year persecution didn't end until well into the twentieth century.

Some Breed Histories
Persians/Angoras

The mysterious feline comes in all shapes and sizes, colors, and temperaments. But until the early 1600's, the only cats seen in Europe, as well as in most parts of the world, were cats with short hair. Imagine the surprise and delight when the first luxurious long-haired felines were encountered.

Part 4

Retractable Claws

Retractable claws are a physical phenomenon that sets cats apart from the rest of the animal kingdom. In the cat family, only cheetahs cannot retract their claws.

The long-haired Persian got its name from its origins in Persia.

As difficult as it is to guess exactly how Persian cats first found their way to civilization, a man named Petro della Valle is accredited with introducing the first long-haired cats into Europe. Della Valle brought several pairs of cats from Persia (known today as Iran) to Italy in approximately 1620. They were named Persians after the area in which they were discovered.

At around the same time, a Frenchman, Nicholas-Claude Fabri de Peiresc, brought long-haired cats from Angora (known today as Ankara), Turkey, back to his homeland. Like the Persians, these cats were dubbed Angoras because of their land of origin.

As we know, most animals in the wild have been able to adapt to all types of cultures and climates. So it is presumed long-haired cats were a result of, or perhaps even a mutation, from crossbreeding between the furry European wild cat and a cat discovered by the German naturalist, Peter Simon Pallas, known as the Steppe Cat.

Long, dense hair was necessary for these felines so they could protect themselves from the cold environments of Persia and Angora. And today, as we brush and groom our long-haired kitties, we must remember they grew these fur coats out of necessity and for the survival of their species.

Part 4

Turkish Van

The Turkish semi-longhair cat is the oldest recorded domesticated semi-longhair and may be the ancestor of all other Northern Hemisphere semi-longhair breeds. Turkish Vans are a rare and ancient breed that developed in central and southwest Asia. "Van" is a common term in the region with Lake Van set roughly in the middle.

In 1955, Laura Lushington and Sonia Halliday were traveling through Turkey and noticed that the cats around the area of Van in Eastern Turkey resembled the traditional Angora type. But these particular cats were different because their coats were not pure white but, instead, included auburn head markings and a faintly ringed auburn tail. Lushington brought two unrelated cats back to Britain, and when they were mated they produced kittens bearing the same auburn markings, thus proving this was a natural breed. She registered the Van name and the Turkish Van became an established breed.

Turkish Vans have a unique cashmere-like texture to their coats that makes their fur water-resistant. An interesting feature of the Turkish Van is that they are fascinated by water. They used lakes and streams to cool down in the hot summers of their native region and have been termed the "swimming" cat by many Van lovers.

American Curl

The American Curl is best known for its unique curled ears, which are the result of a natural mutation. The ears are erect and open; curling away from the cat's face in a graceful arc as opposed to the Scottish Fold's ears, which fold forward and downward. The ears give the breed an alert and happy appearance.

American Curl history is traced back to Lakewood, California. A long-haired, silky black female kitten with unusual ears wandered onto the doorstep of Joe and Grace Ruga. The strange-looking kitten quickly worked her way into the Rugas' hearts and they named her Shulamith, which means "black but comely."

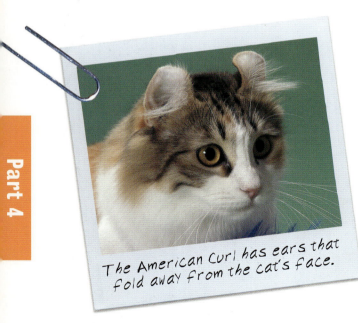

The American Curl has ears that fold away from the cat's face.

Part 4

In December 1981, "Shulamith" delivered her first litter of four kittens. Of the four, two had ears that curled. A geneticist was contacted to study this phenomenon and he confirmed this unusual ear was a genetic trait and was inherited in every case, causing it to be labeled a dominant gene, with no deformities attached to it. Referred to as a spontaneous mutation, the gene that causes the ear to curl appeared to be following a single dominant pattern.

Selective breeding and presentation of the Curls began in 1983, with American Curls officially accepted for CFA registration in 1986, and for championship competition in February 1993. American Curls were also the first breed to be admitted to the Championship Class as one breed with two coat lengths. Recognized as one of the US native American breeds, the American Curl makes a fabulous pet and has remained extremely healthy and hearty with, thankfully, no genetic "defects" associated with that curl gene.

Maine Coon

A Maine Coon cat is a massively-built feline and anyone who has ever seen one will not forget it! But the origins of this "gentle giant," as it has been affectionately called, are still a mystery to many people who have fallen in love with this breed of cat. Because the early Maine Coons were mostly brown tabby in coloring and marking, with darkened rings around their tails, they were thought to resemble a wild raccoon.

From their similarity in appearance, the myth started to spread that this feline, first known of in the mid-1800s, was the result of a raccoon/domestic cat union. However, as experts now know, cross breeding between these two animals is genetically impossible.

We do know the Maine Coon was originally discovered in the state of Maine, where it is known as the official state cat. But before its appearance in Maine, where did this heavily-fur-coated, "wild-looking" cat originate?

The Maine Coon is a beautiful addition to any household.

A popular notion is that the Maine Coon developed from the six domestic, long-haired cats that Marie Antoinette supposedly sent to Maine when she was planning to escape from France during the French Revolution. Of course, she was beheaded before making her escape, but we are indeed fortunate (if the tale is true) that her feline friends crossed the ocean to safety and infinite fame.

The Singapura is the smallest breed of cat. Females weigh between five and six pounds.

British Shorthair

The British Shorthair is a solid and powerful cat with a broad chest and sturdy, strong legs that possesses a quiet demeanor. The breed was developed in Europe from non-pedigreed cats. They are probably the oldest English breed of cat, and can trace their ancestry back to the domestic cat of Rome.

The British Shorthair was first known as the British Blue due to it's original and only recognized color. They became known as the British Shorthair in the 1950s when an assortment of colors was incorporated into the breed. British Shorthairs were also first prized for their physical strength and hunting abilities and were considered Great Britain's "working" cats. Now they are valued family members.

Ragdoll

Ragdolls were developed in the 1960s by California breeder Ann Baker. She bred a cat named Josephine, a loving, gentle, long-haired white Angora carrying Siamese markings, to both a Burmese and Birman male. It was their offspring that resulted in the first Ragdolls. These kittens were blessed with a beautiful nature with the extra qualities of non-matting fur, a huge size, and a non-aggressive disposition.

Ragdolls are slow to mature. It can take between three and four years for Ragdolls to reach full maturity. The Ragdoll is also considered the largest fully-domestic

Did You Know?

The Ragdoll is four to five times heavier than the Singapura, the smallest breed of cat. A female Singapura weighs approximately 5 to 6 pounds, and males weigh 6 to 8 pounds. A Ragdoll can reach over 20 pounds.

Part 4

breed of cat. It reaches its full size and weight at about four years old and neutered males sometimes reach twenty pounds or more.

Independent . . . But Still in Need of Companionship

No matter how independent the feline appears to be, independence does not necessarily equal being a loner. If your animal seems bored or listless, perhaps being an only pet is the problem. Give the single cat a companion or two (or more) of her kind and see how much happier she is.

Whatever breed of cat you own, be sure to give your feline lots of love and care. She will thank you for it.

Kitty will be happy to spend some of her time with her loving owner as well. When she occasionally seems to need her "space," however, try to understand all that the feline species has been through. A little kitty independence and aloofness does not really seem so unreasonable now, does it?

Part 4

Resources

Cat Registry Organizations

Cat registries play an important role in today's world of showing and breeding cats. Most of the registries have stringent rules for accepting particular breeds, making sure they follow the standards set by the association. The following groups are some of the existing associations where cat owners can register their felines.

American Association of Cat Enthusiasts (AACE)

P.O. Box 213

Pine Brook, NJ 07058

Phone: (973) 335-6717

Website: http://www.aaceinc.org

American Cat Fanciers Association (ACFA)

P.O. Box 1949

Nixa, MO 65714

Phone: (417) 725-1530

Website: http://www.acfacat.com

Canadian Cat Association (CCA)

289 Rutherford Road South

Unit 18

Brampton, Ontario, Canada L6W 3R9

Phone: (905) 459-1481

Website: http://www.cca-afc.com

The Cat Fanciers' Association (CFA)

1805 Atlantic Avenue

P.O. Box 1005

Manasquan, NJ 08736-0805

Phone: (732) 528-9797

Website: http://www.cfainc.org

Cat Fanciers' Federation (CFF)

P.O. Box 661

Gratis, OH 45330

Phone: (937) 787-9009

Website: http://www.cffinc.org

Fédération Internationale Féline (FIFe)

Penelope Bydlinski, General Secretary

Little Dene, Lenham Heath

Maidstone, Kent, ME17 2BS ENGLAND

Phone: +44 1622 850913

Website: http://www.fifeweb.org

The Governing Council of the Cat Fancy (GCCF)

4-6, Penel Orlieu

Bridgwater, Somerset, TA6 3PG UK

Phone: +44 (0)1278 427 575

Website: http://ourworld.compuserve.com/home-pages/GCCF_CATS/

The International Cat Association (TICA)

P.O. Box 2684

Harlingen, TX 78551

Phone: (956) 428-8046

Website: http://www.tica.org

Traditional and Classic Cat International (TCCI)

(formerly known as the Traditional Cat Association)

10289 Vista Point Loop

Penn Valley, CA 95946

Website: http://www.tccat.org

Cat-Related Websites

Most cat owners are always looking for ways to enhance their beloved's pet's life as well as find answers to the many questions of "Why does my cat do that?" Your world is now much simpler thanks to the Internet. If you have a question to ask, a story to share, a problem to overcome, or just want to spend hours surfing the 'net looking at cat photos, reading cat behavior articles, or looking at the newest in cool, cat-related clothing, you won't have to go any further than your computer.

Acme Pet Feline Guide

(http://www.acmepet.com/feline/index.html)

A leading figure in the pet products industry, Acme Pet has put together an extensive site. At the feline site, you can access the feline marketplace, which has places to shop for cat products as well as a pet library, reference materials and articles, questions and answers about cats, an extensive list of rescue organizations, clubs and shelters, and the ever popular "cat chat" room.

Cat Collectors

(http://www.catcollectors.com)

This club is designed for people who collect cat-related items (such as figurines, books, artwork, advertisements, and other items that bear a cat motif), and is the first of its kind. Club founder, Marilyn Dipboye, started Cat Collectors in 1982 so that the people who enjoy this hobby can network with each other, whether selling or trading certain pieces or just sharing friendships. A newsletter, *Cat Talk,* is mailed bi-monthly to its members.

Cat Fanciers Website

(http://www.fanciers.com)

In 1993, the Cat Fanciers mailing list was started on the Internet as an open forum for breeders, exhibitors, judges, or anyone interested in the world of the Cat Fancy. The on-line discussion group has thousands of members from all over the world. The group's focus, however, is to make life better for felines around the globe. The site offers general information on cat shows, breed descriptions, veterinary resources, and much more.

The Daily Cat

(http://www.thedailycat.com)
The Daily Cat is a resource for cats and their owners. The site provides information on feline health, care, nutrition, grooming, and behavior.

Healthypet

(http://www.healthypet.com)
Healthypet.com is part of the American Animal Hospital Association, an organization of more than 25,000 veterinary care providers committed to providing excellence in small animal care.

Petfinder

(http://www.petfinder.org)
On Petfinder.org, you can search over 88,000 adoptable animals and locate shelters and rescue groups in your area who are currently caring for adoptable pets. You can also post classified ads for lost or found pets, pets wanted, and pets needing homes.

Pets 911

(http://www.1888pets911.org)
Pets 911 is not only a website, but also runs a toll-free phone hotline (1-888-PETS-911) that allows pet owners access to important, life-saving information.

ShowCatsOnline

(http://www.showcatsonline.com)
ShowCatsOnline.com is an online magazine devoted to all breeds of pedigreed cats. They provide information on the breeding and showing of all breeds of pedigreed cats and update their members on the latest developments in medical care, breeding, grooming, and showing.

21cats.org

(http://21cats.org)
21Cats provides information that will help cats live longer, healthier lives. The site contains online Health and Care InfoCenter, an 'Ask the Kitty Nurse' Hotline, and a free monthly newsletter. One of their goals is to raise awareness of successful methods used to reduce the cat overpopulation problem.

VetQuest

(http://www.vin.com/vetquest/index0.html)
VetQuest is an online veterinary search and referral service. You can search their database for over 25,000 Veterinary Hospitals and Clinics in the United States, Canada, and Europe. The service places special emphasis on veterinarians with advanced online access to the latest health care information and highly qualified veterinary specialists and consultants.

These cat-related websites are only a handful of feline sites you can check out to learn a thing or two about your faithful friend. Good luck surfing the web for anything and everything "CAT!"

Cat-Related Publications

(Subscription contact information)

You love your cat and you love to read. There are a variety of magazines and newsletters devoted to caring for and understanding living with felines. Subscribe to any of these magazines and get ready to read educational, funny, and heartwarming articles and stories about cats!

Animal Wellness Magazine
PMB 168
8174 South Holly Street
Centennial, CO 80122

ASPCA Animal Watch
424 East 92nd Street
New York, NY 10128

Best Friends Magazine
Best Friends Animal Sanctuary
Kanab, UT 84741

Cat Fancy Magazine
P.O. Box 52864
Boulder, CO 80322

Catnip
P.O. Box 420070
Palm Coast, FL 32142

CatWatch
P.O. Box 420235
Palm Coast, FL 32142

PetLife Magazine
P.O. Box 500
Missouri, TX 77549

Whole Cat Journal
P.O. Box 1337
Radford, VA 24143

Your Cat Magazine
1716 Locust Street
Des Moines, IA 50309

Veterinarian Specialty/Membership Organizations

There are many organizations that your veterinarian might have a membership in as we l as special veterinary associations you can search to locate a doctor in your area or to help you with a specific pet ailment.

American Animal Hospital Association (AAHA)
P.O. Box 150899
Denver, CO 80215
Phone: (303) 986-2800
Website: http://www.aahanet.org

American Association of Feline Practitioners (AAFP)
200 4th Avenue North, Suite 900
Nashville, TN 37219
Phone: (615) 259-7788
Toll-free: (800) 204-3514
Website: http://www.aafponline.org

American Board of Veterinary Practitioners (ABVP)

200 4th Avenue North, Suite 900

Nashville, TN 37219

Phone: (615) 254-3687

Fax: (615) 254-7047

Website: http://www.abvp.com

American College of Veterinary Preventive Medicine (ACVPM)

3126 Morning Creek

San Antonio, TX 78247

Website: http://www.acvpm.org

American Holistic Veterinary Medical Association (AHVMA)

2214 Old Emmorton Road

Bel Air, MD 21015

Phone: (410) 569-0795

Website: http://www.ahvma.org

American Veterinary Medical Association (AVMA)

1931 North Meacham Road, Suite 100

Schaumburg, IL 60173

Phone: (847) 925-8070

Fax: (847) 925-1329

Website: http://www.avma.org

The Academy of Veterinary Homeopathy (AVH)

P.O. Box 9280

Wilmington, DE 19809

Phone: (866) 652-1590

Website: http://www.theavh.org

The American Association for Veterinary Acupuncture (AAVA)

P.O. Box 419

Hygiene, CO 80533

Phone: (303) 772-6726

Website: http://www.aava.org

Cornell Feline Health Center

College of Veterinary Medicine

Cornell University, Box 13

Ithaca, NY 14853

Phone: (607) 253-3414

Website:
http://web.vet.cornell.edu/public/fhc/FelineHealth.html

International Veterinary Acupuncture Society (IVAS)

P.O. Box 271395

Ft. Collins, CO 80527

Phone: (970) 266-0666

Website: http://www.ivas.org

Animal Welfare Groups and Organizations

Many cat welfare societies, such as the Humane Society of the United States (HSUS) and American Society for the Prevention of Cruelty to Animals (ASPCA), exist as protection and information agencies for pets. Although the groups have various objectives, they all have one goal: to protect cats, as well as all animals, from abuse and neglect. It is impossible to list all the societies that protect pets, but the following list provides a place to start.

Alley Cat Allies
1801 Belmont Road NW, Suite 201
Washington, DC 20009
Phone: (202) 667-3630
Website: http://www.alleycat.org

American Humane Association (AHA)
63 Inverness Drive East
Englewood, CO 80112
Phone: (800) 227-4645
Website: http://www.americanhumane.org

American Society for the Prevention of Cruelty to Animals (ASPCA)
424 East 92 Street
New York, NY 10128
Phone: (212) 876-7700
Website: http://www.aspca.org

Best Friends Animal Sanctuary
Kanab, UT 84741-5001
Phone: (435) 644-2001
Website: http://www.bestfriends.org

Cats Protection
17 Kings Road
Horsham, West Sussex RH13 5PN UK
Phone: +44 (0) 1403 221900
Website: http://www.cats.org.uk

Feral Cat Coalition
9528 Miramar Road, PMB 160
San Diego, CA 92126
Phone: (619) 497-1599
Website: http://www.feralcat.com

The Fund For Animals
200 West 57th Street
New York, NY 10019
Phone: (212) 246-2096
Website: http://www.fund.org

The Humane Society of the United States (HSUS)
2100 L Street, NW
Washington, DC 20037
Phone: (212) 452-1100
Website: http://www.hsus.org

North Shore Animal League (NSAL)
25 Davis Avenue
Port Washington, NY 11050
Phone: (516) 883-7575
Website: http://www.nsal.org

The Winn Feline Foundation, Inc.
1805 Atlantic Avenue
P.O. Box 1005
Manasquan, NJ 08736-0805
Phone: (732) 528-9797
Website: http://www.winnfelinehealth.org

Index

Photo Credits

Joan Balzarini: 20, 32, 36, 49, 59 (bottom), 65, 74, 140, 193, 196 (top), 197, 205, 217 (top)

Linda Beatie: 59 (top), 75 (bottom), 114

Richard K. Blackmon: 116 (top), 126, 127 (top), 128, 141 (bottom), 188

Albert Connelly: 92, 173

Jacquie DeLillo: 19 (top), 27, 53 (top), 96

Isabelle Francais: 17 (top), 23, 28, 29 (top), 30, 35, 38-42, 43 (bottom), 44 (top), 45-47, 50, 52 (bottom), 53 (bottom), 55, 57, 63 (top), 64 (bottom), 68, 84 (top), 86, 89, 90 (top), 91, 94 (top), 95, 97-101, 104, 106, 108, 110, 112, 113, 116 (bottom), 117, 118, 120 (bottom), 121 (bottom), 130 (bottom), 133, 139, 153 (top and bottom), 154, 155, 159-161, 163, 164, 166, 168, 170 (top), 174, 176, 185, 189, 195, 199, 200, 202 (top), 207-209, 211 (top), 213, 216, 219, 220, 222

M. Gilroy: 132 (bottom)

Mary Ann Kahn: 175

Stuart Levine: 98, 125, 221

Gillian Lisle: 15, 17 (bottom), 21, 29 (bottom), 33, 61, 87 (right), 111, 136, 156, 181, 212, 223

William Mara: 120 (top)

Nikki Munger: 217 (bottom)

Robert Pearcy: 1, 19 (bottom), 22 (top and bottom), 25, 31, 37 (bottom), 43 (top), 44 (bottom), 62, 67 (top and bottom), 71, 76, 77, 78, 80, 82, 84 (bottom), 85, 87 (left), 127 (bottom), 129, 131, 137, 138 (top), 141 (top), 143, 147, 150, 158, 165, 177, 182, 183 (bottom), 186 (top), 190 (left), 196 (bottom), 198, 210 (bottom), 211 (bottom), 218

Ron Regan: 135, 210 (top)

Adrienne Rescinio: 26, 184

Toni Rogers: 203

Vince Serbin: 16, 18, 115, 122, 130 (top), 138 (bottom), 187 (top), 190 (right), 194 (bottom), 202 (bottom)

Lara Stern: 105, 121 (top), 134, 149, 157, 178, 179

Linda Sturdy: 102, 183 (top), 186 (bottom), 194 (top), 204

Karen Taylor: 72

Candida M. Tomassini: 60

John Tyson: 52 (top), 63 (bottom), 64 (top), 73 (top and bottom), 75 (top), 90 (bottom), 94 (bottom), 132 (top), 145, 146, 148, 170 (bottom), 201

Kelli A. Wilkins: 37 (top), 83, 187 (bottom), 215

Cartoons by Michael Pifer